Art Deco Interiors

Art Deco Interiors

Decoration and Design Classics of the 1920s and 1930s

PATRICIA BAYER

THAMES AND HUDSON

For Michael Goldman

Frontispiece
Lobby of the Chrysler Building, New York, 1927-30
(photo Norman McGrath)

© 1990 Thames and Hudson Ltd, London

Published in paperback in the United States of America in 1998 by
Thames and Hudson Inc., 500 Fifth Avenue, New York, New York 10110

Library of Congress Catalog Card Number 97-61367
ISBN 0-500-28020-7

Printed and bound in Singapore

CONTENTS

Dining Room by Emile-Jacques Ruhlmann, from his pavilion at the 1925 Paris Exposition

INTRODUCTION

During the period between *c.*1910 and 1939, the multifaceted design style known as Art Deco took root, blossomed, flourished and faded, only to be revived again, as are most classics sooner or later, in the recent past. From its rich Parisian beginnings – pure, high-style Art Deco – to its jazzy, Streamline Moderne American offshoots, Art Deco has come to be viewed as the most exciting decorative style of the century, introducing or utilizing such diverse elements as the richly lacquered, Oriental-style screen; the sleek, tubular-steel chair; the ebony-veneered, ivory-dotted writing desk; the vivid, geometric-patterned carpet; the sunburst-decorated stained-glass window; the starkly angular ceiling or wall light fixture; the classically or coquettishly draped glass figurine; the stylized ceramic polar bear. It also ushered in the era of the 'total' interior.

The Exposition Internationale des Arts Décoratifs et Industriels Modernes, the world's fair held in Paris in 1925 and from which the style derives its name (although the term 'Art Deco' did not come into widespread use until the late 1960s), played a central and crucial role in dictating the appearance of the Art Deco interior. Not only did the Exposition feature the works of Ruhlmann, Süe et Mare, Chareau and others, but it also represented the apogee of pure French Art Deco – an opulent, luxuriant design style whose own origins extended as far back as the eighteenth century, appropriately enough to the great French *ébénistes* such as Jean-Henri Riesener and Charles Cressent; it also recognized the influence of African tribal art, Japanese lacquer-work, contemporary abstract painting and sculpture, and diverse other elements.

In truth, the Art Deco interior is many things to many people, and even in its country of origin it was a horse of variegated colours. There were the opulent, plush salons of antiquity-inspired Armand-Albert Rateau and Ballets Russes-influenced Paul Poiret, dripping with tassels, awash with puffy pillows and floor cushions, and punctuated by exotic, often glittering, patterns on walls, floors and screens; there were also starker Modernist settings, for example, by Le Corbusier, Charlotte Perriand and Eileen Gray, with their chromed-metal and leather chaises-longues, pure-white walls, sleek modern floors covered with carpets woven with complementary geometric motifs, and simple, squared-off end tables, surmounted perhaps by abstract or primitive sculptures. And there was a host of permutations in between, incorporating elements of the opulent Deco and the minimal Moderne, making new and exciting statements, borrowing from past sources and exotic cultures.

Art Deco went one step beyond its immediate predecessor, Art Nouveau, which was the first style to break with the repetition, redundancy and sheer weight and dullness of its late-nineteenth-century contemporaries. Art Deco was the first truly modern style of interior decoration in its use of new technologies and materials, in thrall to traditional craftsmen as well as talented emergent industrial designers, making simpler, more practical furniture for smaller rooms. Its exponents broke barriers, embraced innovation, honoured the past, but most of all put together the elements of a room, a whole apartment or house, a cinema or theatre, a hotel or an ocean liner, in a thoughtful, dynamic, integrated way, employing a kind of *gesamtkunstwerk* design methodology which at its best resulted in a unified, handsome whole.

The classic elegance and good taste of high-style Art Deco can best be seen in the outstanding Parisian interiors of the 1920s (and, to a lesser degree, the late 1910s and early 1930s), which were often the collaborative effort of furniture and textile designers, painters and sculptors, and an array of other artists and craftsmen. It was during this fecund interwar period that the *ensemblier* came to prominence, with such notables as Emile-Jacques Ruhlmann, Eileen Gray, Jules Leleu, Maurice Dufrêne (for La Maîtrise), Paul Follot (for Pomone), and Süe et Mare's Compagnie des Arts Français being commissioned to create the total design of a room, in other words, its *ensemble* – from floor to ceiling, side table to settee, ashtray to chandelier.

The Art Deco interior in the United States was at times a reflection of its high-style Parisian counterpart – with gleaming lacquered surfaces, plump *fauteuil* chairs and stylized floral motifs – and at times a mirror-image of the functionalism of Le Corbusier or Marcel Breuer. But there developed a distinctly American Art Deco hybrid in the late 1920s and 1930s which was largely indebted, if not to indigenous, at least to recently transplanted sources – these ranging from the glitzy Hollywood set to the glittering Manhattan skyline, from the streamlined, aerodynamic forms of nascent industrial design to modern developments in plastics and other synthetic substances. Designers like Donald Deskey, Paul T. Frankl, Wolfgang Hoffmann, Winold Reiss, Gilbert Rohde, Eliel Saarinen, Eugene Schoen and Kem Weber – many of these recent *émigrés* from a strife-torn Europe – applied their talents to creating interiors for a wealthy, discerning clientele.

Then, too, there were the often massive public spaces these and other notables were commissioned to design and furnish: hotel and restaurant interiors, the lobbies of office buildings, the waiting rooms of airports and railroad terminals, the auditoriums of ever-increasing, ever more lavish movie houses, often known as, appropriately, 'picture palaces'. There were also the interiors that filtered down to the Middle American mass market, usually dining-, living- and bedroom suites containing watered-down elements of Art Deco and combined with mass-produced lamps, carpets, and other room fixtures and accessories, the occupants having been inspired, perhaps, by a recent excursion to the cinema, or a browse through one of the popular home-decoration magazines that were published, such as *House and Garden* and *Good Furniture*.

Eileen Gray put together this casual, multipurpose living room for E.1027, Jean Badovici's house in the south of France, built in 1929. The rugs and chairs ('Bibendum' left, 'Transat' right) are Gray designs. A large marine chart decorates the walls.

The English Art Deco interior is often popularly seen as an everyday 1930s sitting room, something that would have been found in an Ideal Home exhibition – complete with cheerful, overstuffed settee and chairs, boxy wireless, geometric throw-rugs, gleaming electric fire and brightly patterned curtains outdone by an even more vividly hued tea set displayed in a glass-doored cabinet. But there were also domestic and public spaces in Britain which could hold their own with some of the most notable Art Deco interiors of Paris and New York. Many a British Odeon or other cinema, for instance, boasted splendid décors, ranging from the most subtle Streamline Moderne to the most lavishly ornamented baroque.

The authentic Art Deco interior was also created in countries far away from Europe and North America. Often such spaces were designed by Europeans (or designers educated abroad), or at least largely furnished with Continental pieces, and many of them, having been commissioned by necessarily ultra-wealthy clients, were prime examples of high-style Paris-inspired Art Deco.

In the 1970s and 1980s, numerous architects, designers, decorators and collectors began to devote their energies and apply their skills (or, in the case of the latter, empty their wallets) to the end of achieving an Art Deco-style interior. The elegance and classicism of this style appealed to a new generation, tired perhaps of the postwar-practical followed by Op Art-Psychedelic designs of the fifties and sixties, and desirous of a return to beauty, or at least a dramatic sea change from what they were used to, what they had grown up with. As designs seem to take a half century or so to be fully appreciated, assessed and consequently revived, the 1970s was the time for 1920s Art Deco to come into its own.

At the same time, many authentic Art Deco interiors – those which had not been senselessly demolished by unthinking building developers – were dusted off, shined up or otherwise restored to their original elegance. Sometimes period interiors were enhanced with contemporary touches, which were in part an homage to Art Deco but at the same time very much of the present in conception and execution. The extensive 1979-83 renovation of Unilever House in London, masterminded by Theo Crosby of Pentagram Design, is a superb example of a modern refurbishment of an Art Deco building. The Post-Modern creations of the Memphis Group and of such architects and designers as Michael Graves, Hans Hollein, Andrée Putman and Charles Jencks – though decidedly of the here and now – nonetheless pay tribute to the Art Deco past, and in some avant-garde interiors coexist quite comfortably with their ancestors in design from earlier in the century.

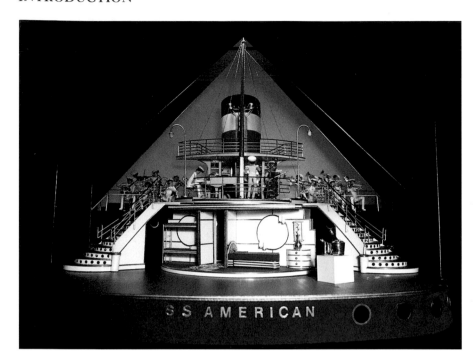

A chic shipboard interior (*left*) in the 1930s mode was created in the late 1980s by stage and film set designer Tony Walton, for the London revival of the Cole Porter musical *Anything Goes*.

The 1929-30 Pantages Theater in Los Angeles (B. Marcus Priteca, architect) (*below*) was one of America's most dazzling cinemas, with a fretwork of sunrays and scrolls surrounding a massive chandelier and a wealth of classic Art Deco motifs – blossoms, volutes, lightning bolts – around the glittering auditorium.

Multi-talented industrial designer Raymond Loewy conceived this streamlined, cool-toned bar car (*left*) for the Pennsylvania Railroad's *Broadway Limited* in 1937.

The private bar was one of the new elements to be found in domestic Art Deco interiors (*below left*). This mid-1930s English model – mainly of black and primrose Vitrolite (an opaque coloured glass) – was designed by Kenneth Cheesman and made by the British Vitrolite Company.

The interiors of London's Unilever House (*below*) were in large part restored by Theo Crosby of the design firm Pentagram in 1979-83. Exuberant lighting fixtures and capitals, among other decorative elements, were added to the entrance hall.

A French Art Deco influence can be seen in the pillow-laden divan (*left*), but the glittering screen and stepped sconces are more American, specifically, Hollywood: the film is *Our Dancing Daughters* (1928, Cedric Gibbons, art director).

The stylized floral forms of the metalwork, the geometric design on the pelmet and the gleaming tubular metal of the furniture combined to make the Wonder Bar cocktail lounge, in St Louis's Roosevelt Hotel (*below left*), a smartly Moderne meeting place.

English designer Betty Joel produced these handsome pieces (*below*), part of a sycamore bedroom suite from 1929 and one of her many practical but attractive interiors designed with the working woman in mind. Note the emphatic patterns on the wood veneer, a Joel speciality.

New York's Aschermann Studio designed this space for a bachelor's home in Forest Hills, Long Island. With its subtle floral highlights and largely rectilinear forms, this blue- and black-dominated dining room (*above*) is highly reminiscent of earlier Vienna Secession interiors.

Walter Gropius, founder of the Bauhaus, created this austere, eminently functional lady's bedroom (*left*) in 1926 at Dessau. Decorative elements are non-existent, even around the dressing table.

CHAPTER 1
THE ART DECO INTERIOR
ORIGINS AND INFLUENCES

During the years from 1910 to 1915, design in much of Europe, including Paris, was still disentangling itself from the lingering tendrils of Art Nouveau and earlier, largely historicizing styles. But a group of far-seeing Parisian designers were already looking to a wide range of sources for inspiration, both traditional and contemporary, European and exotic, in the development of a modern and original design style. Indeed, a handful of these figures had worked and even flourished in the Art Nouveau era, but the new century saw the languorous S-curves and nature-inspired motifs of that movement give way to more stylized lines and formalized motifs.

At the turn of the century, two European cities, Glasgow and Vienna, greatly helped to set the stage for Art Deco, both producing proto-modern furniture, objects and interiors that made use of elements which found their way into subsequent French (not to mention other European and American) design. The work of the Glasgow designers, notably of Charles Rennie Mackintosh (1868-1928), was in fact much admired by the Viennese Secessionists, and it is not difficult to discern similar concerns and sensibilities at work in the interiors created by Josef Hoffmann (1870-1956), Koloman Moser (1868-1918), Adolf Loos (1870-1933), Otto Wagner (1841-1918), Joseph Maria Olbrich (1867-1908), Otto Prutscher (1880-1949) and other Austrians. Just as the designers of the Glasgow School were dissatisfied with the largely retrospective and cluttered Victorian interiors that made up most British homes, so too were the Secessionists desirous of parting with dusty tradition and breaking off from the artistic establishment, not only in terms of architecture and decoration, but painting and sculpture as well (Gustav Klimt was one of their key members). On the whole, typical Vienna Secession interiors were spare, severe and geometric, but a glorious exception to this rule, the magnificent Palais Stoclet (1905-11) in Brussels, boasted an interior of a richness, elegance and harmony that was almost more Oriental than Western, more Parisian than Viennese, in its overall grandeur.

Somewhat akin to both the Vienna Secession designers and those of the Glasgow School were certain Scandinavian designers of the early twentieth century, notably Eliel Saarinen (1873-1950), who in fact emigrated to the United States in 1923, eventually becoming director of the influential Cranbrook Academy of Art in Michigan. These early interiors of Saarinen were light, airy and simple, containing largely rectilinear furnishings. German Jugendstil interiors of the early twentieth century were related stylistically to such Northern European (and Viennese and Glaswegian) designs, often making use of light-hued furniture (some built-in) of clean, straight lines, and wall, floor and window decorations with complementary colours and designs.

The Glaswegian and Viennese designs that served as harbingers of Parisian Art Deco were immediate, direct sources, but other origins of the style were more indirect. The exotic roots of Art Deco – those that emanated from the Orient, from ancient Egypt and from classical antiquity – were already firmly ensconced in the annals of design and had inspired Europeans for generations. But in the twentieth century such sources were approached from different angles and in a new light, and the resultant designs they inspired were more often than not distinctively modern and stylized. Oriental art and decoration had long proved an inspiration to Western designers, their motifs and methods used in furniture and pottery. Art Deco designers in their turn looked to the East for both subject matter and production techniques, including lacquering, and in some cases Eastern natives actually taught Occidentals, thus directly spreading their knowledge throughout the West.

The papyri, lotus blossoms and scarab beetles of Pharaonic Egypt also appeared in certain strains of Art Deco, but less so in the Parisian than in the British and American. In part inspired by Howard Carter's 1922 discovery of Tutankhamen's tomb, the Egyptomania of the 1920s (not the revival's first reincarnation, of course) was well suited to public spaces such as cinemas and restaurants, and also to personal adornments, like jewellery and handbags. Another ancient civilization, that of the Mayas in Central America, also influenced design in the 1920s, especially in the United States, where stylistic elements relating to the stepped pyramid and outer decoration of Mayan, and later Aztec, temples found their way on to numerous buildings and objects, notably – and appropriately – the stepped exteriors of urban skyscrapers.

Neoclassicism also provided some of the design vocabulary of Art Deco, although it was not among the style's primary influences. Most taken with motifs of these imperial eras were the Parisian metalworkers and designers in metal – not surprisingly, since patinated bronze was such a significant component of so many of the furnishings of antiquity. Its best-known exponent was Armand-Albert Rateau, whose decorative pieces and entire interiors – many of the latter commissioned by the fashion designer Jeanne Lanvin – echoed the glories of ancient Rome.

Another foreign influence on Art Deco designers, especially those in Paris, was tribal Africa, a source of inspiration as well to many of the abstract artists of the early twentieth century. African art began to be collected in great quantities at this time, so it is not surprising that Art Deco designers adapted the 'primitive' forms of the masks, furniture and ritual objects of African tribes to their own modern tastes. Pierre Legrain (1869-1929), for instance, one of the multitalented individuals commissioned by couturier Jacques Doucet to design objects for his collection, reproduced African forms in his furniture. International exhibitions like the Exposition Coloniale, held in Paris in 1931, provided additional sources of inspiration to designers taken with the sensuous forms, materials and subject matter of Africa.

The 1905-11 Palais Stoclet, Brussels, whose decoration was supervised by Josef Hoffmann and realized by the Wiener Werkstätte, boasted interiors of a richness, elegance and harmony more Parisian than Viennese, indeed more Oriental than European. The hall's floors and walls are patterned and inlaid marble, the woodwork is palissander, and the sofa and chairs are covered in deerskin.

A significant impact on Parisian Art Deco, and consequently on manifestations of the style in other countries, was made by the exuberant, colourful and at times joyfully naïve costumes and stage sets of the Ballets Russes, which first performed in the French capital in 1909. Indeed, the 1905 exhibition of Fauvist painting at the Salon d'Automne had already set Paris areel with its profusion of bright colours, so it was not surprising that the Russian palette had such a strong effect. The sheer sensuous Orientalism of the company took the city by storm, but this was an unabashed, wildly spirited brand of Eastern ritual and design, quite dissimilar to the refined sensibilities of the Japanese, who were soon to work their spell over Eileen Gray and Jean Dunand.

The art, architecture and design movements of De Stijl, Futurism, Constructivism and the Bauhaus may at first seem at odds with Art Deco, yet elements of these (and of other, splinter groups) could be found in the more refined, rectilinear, Modernist manifestations of Parisian design. De Stijl, the Dutch movement (and magazine) whose major exponents were painters Theo van Doesburg and Piet Mondrian, architects J. J. Oud and Jan Wils, and designer Gerrit Rietveld, was a style whose aim was to address itself to all segments of contemporary culture, including fine art, architecture, design and poetry, and to create homogeneous interiors, exteriors and objects sympathetic to their goal of an artistic unity. The designs of De Stijl, especially those for furniture, proved an inspiration to members of the Bauhaus, the multidisciplinary design school founded by Walter Gropius in Weimar, Germany, in 1919, and whose credo centred on a unity of the arts, on guild-like work methods and on practical, functional construction. Marcel Breuer was one of the first Bauhaus students, and many of his earlier chair designs show a debt to Rietveld's creations. By the mid 1920s, after the Bauhaus had moved to Dessau, their furniture and objects took on altogether more geometric proportions, and also came to be made of new materials, such as tubular steel, more suitable for mass production, to which the Bauhaus was committed. Another important point to make about the Bauhaus in relation to Art Deco is that the German school attempted to unite the various design disciplines, producing as it did furniture, ceramics, textiles, glass and metalwork. The Bauhaus interior, whoever it was who put it together, represented a harmony or totality of design, with all the furnishings relating to each other and contributing to a unified whole.

Although Futurism and Constructivism, the Italian and Russian art movements, had little bearing on Art Deco per se, they nonetheless contributed to aspects of the style as a whole. Futurism, for instance, so enamoured of modernity and speed, can be seen as a direct antecedent of the aerodynamic shapes in the work of many of America's industrial designers, such as Raymond Loewy and Walter Dorwin Teague. Likewise Constructivism, which grew out of the art of collage and was all but finished as a movement in the early 1920s, contributed ideas – and designers – to French and other European design of the time. The combined use of often unusual materials was one concern of this radical group, and László Moholy-Nagy, the Hungarian Constructivist who later taught at the Bauhaus, was especially committed to the use of Perspex and chromed metal (he also created the metal-heavy sets for the 1936 film *Things to Come*).

Mention should also be made of the English Arts and Crafts Movement which, although founded on and operated along the lines of idealistic, medievalist beliefs, practices and organization, could also be said to have exerted some influence on Art Deco. It did so, however, in a fairly third-hand, indirect manner, inspiring as it did the Deutscher Werkbund and the Bauhaus, two German design schools whose *modi operandi* were rooted in those of the Arts and Crafts Movement, and whose creations and methods in turn had immediate effects on French designers. In fact, the Deutscher Werkbund (founded in Munich in 1907, with Hermann Muthesius at its helm) was represented in the 1910 Salon d'Automne and received much praise for its 'intelligent co-operation of businessmen and artists', as well as its eclectic display of furniture, from the strict shapes of Richard Riemerschmid's pieces to the elegant, even luxuriant forms of Bruno Paul's designs. Several important Art Deco designers in the United States, including Scandinavian-born Eliel Saarinen and the great Prairie School architect-designer, Frank Lloyd Wright (who might also be considered the premier American *ensemblier*, though his 'ensembles' were radically different from those of Parisian designers), adhered to Arts and Crafts-based aesthetics during their careers.

All these contemporary – and roughly contemporaneous – movements, schools and individuals aside, however, it must be stated that high-style Parisian Art Deco – the Art Deco of Ruhlmann, Süe et Mare, Groult, Lalique and others – was perhaps most strongly influenced by an equally high-style past, most notably of France, for the firmest, deepest roots of the Art Deco *ensembliers* were in the eighteenth-century. Many of the forms, techniques, motifs and materials used by the Parisian *ensembliers* referred back to earlier Gallic styles. The grand furniture and interiors by Emile-Jacques Ruhlmann especially echoed the works of his eighteenth-century predecessors, although they were never conscious, deliberate reproductions of classic pieces, but more an homage to the furniture makers and designers of the Louis Quinze and Louis Seize styles.

Diaghilev's Ballets Russes, from their Paris début in 1909 – with their bold hues, vibrant patterns and overall Oriental splendour – wove a spell over French designers, both of fashion and interiors. Léon Bakst's design for *La Pisanella* exemplifies the Russian company's colourful exoticism.

The allure and influence of Pharaonic Egypt have been strong throughout the ages, as these three images show. The nineteenth-century French lithograph (*right*), following in the wake of Napoleon's Egyptian campaign, presents an artist's colourful rendering of an interior in a wealthy ancient Egyptian household. The black-and-white photograph (*above right*) is of a neo-ancient-Egyptian lounge on the British vessel the *Monarch of Bermuda*, its scarab, papyrus and other motifs undoubtedly influenced by the 1922 discovery of the tomb of Tutankhamen. The modern dining area (*above*) is in Unilever House, London, a 1931 building whose interiors were in large part designed in the 1980s by Theo Crosby in a contemporary mode sympathetic to the period setting.

Emile-Jacques Ruhlmann, the premier Art Deco furniture and interior designer, looked to his classic Gallic predecessors for many of his forms, which he then duly updated. This delicate day-bed, with a tasselled bolster pillow at either end (*opposite*), is reminiscent of an Empire-style *canapé*, and the entire ensemble constitutes an elegant, rarefied milieu of timeless good taste.

At the 1921 Salon d'Automne in Paris, this elegant ensemble (*top*) – evocative of the Empire period in its delicate forms and floral motifs – was displayed by Messrs Gallot, Dufour et Roussin. The room is far less stylized than those by Ruhlmann and other well-known *ensembliers* and relies more on traditional forms.

The graceful forms of the lacquer-red chairs, the delicate floral designs on the walls, the pastel hues and the fretwork grille on the right give this *c.* 1929 German dining room (*centre*), in a villa at Lake Starnberg, an Oriental look. The lamps add a jaunty modern touch.

Maurice Dufrêne was one of several designers whose career began in the Art Nouveau period and who made a successful transition to *le style 1925*. This 1906 Dufrêne bedroom (*right*) still adheres in the main to an Art Nouveau vocabulary, but exhibits traces of his later, more restrained style.

The highly functional, primary-coloured but somewhat uncomfortable De Stijl interiors, such as this one in Gerrit Rietveld's 1924-25 Schröder House in Utrecht (*above*), could not have been more at odds with the opulent, high-style confections of French Art Deco. But its revolutionary aspects, such as movable partitions and multi purpose furniture, were to have a much greater effect on subsequent interior design.

Concurrent with decorative Parisian Art Deco was the strictly functional, Dutch-originated De Stijl movement. Félix Del Marle was one of its French exponents, and his 1926 suite of furniture for a 'Madame B.' in Dresden – seen in a vintage black-and-white (*above left*) and modern colour photograph (*left*) – was called by Piet Mondrian, the premier De Stijl painter, 'the best application of Neo-Plasticism'.

Frank Lloyd Wright applied his immense talent not only to the exteriors of buildings, but also to their harmonious interiors. His 1923 textile-block Storer House (*above*), in Los Angeles, was restored in the 1980s. Although the architect did not in fact design any furniture for the house, today it is filled with original pieces by the master and his son, Lloyd Wright.

23

Charles Rennie Mackintosh, although best known for his light-hued interiors filled with subtly rectilinear dark-veneered or white-painted furniture, also created strikingly modern, starkly geometric spaces, such as this bedroom of 1915-17 (*left*) in the Bassett-Lowke House, Northampton. The room embodies that Viennese strain of Modernism marked by straight lines, chequerboard motifs and a minimum of ornament – a strong influence on the vocabulary of Art Deco.

The unembellished, tubular-metal-dominated interiors of the Bauhaus school were to have a long-lasting effect on Western design. The dining alcove and sitting area in Mies van der Rohe's Tugendhat House (1928-30)(*below*), in Brno, Czechoslovakia, are as timeless – and international – as the Barcelona and other chairs that fill them.

The arts of tribal Africa were widely displayed, appreciated and collected in Paris in the 1920s and 1930s. They also proved inspirational to a host of designers, among them Eyre de Lanux and Evelyn Wyld, whose African-flavoured *c.* 1931 bed, table and rugs – in neutral shades of cream, tan, brick and grey – are shown (*left*).

The influence of Hoffmann, Moser and other Vienna Secessionists was far-reaching. Their chequerboard and dotted motifs, among others, can be seen in this 1915-18 interior design (*below*), probably for a fabric or wallpaper shop; it was executed by Winold Reiss, a New Yorker who emigrated from Germany to the United States in 1913.

The Grand Salon of Emile-Jacques Ruhlmann's Hôtel du Collectionneur pavilion
at the 1925 Paris Exposition.

CHAPTER 2
SHOWCASE INTERIORS
THE GREAT EXHIBITIONS

As with no other preceding artistic style, images of Art Deco were disseminated throughout Europe, North America and the rest of the world by a variety of media, means and forums. From international exhibitions and salons, which were reviewed extensively in the ever-growing printed press and often accompanied by black-and-white photographs, to limited-edition albums and portfolios, Art Deco reached out to influence designers and consumers the world over – an influence which reached its peak at the Paris Exposition of 1925.

As early as 1901, in fact, only a year after the Paris Exposition Universelle had presented Art Nouveau at its apogee (in addition to a plethora of insignificant regional movements and designs), a group of designers formed the Société des Artistes Décorateurs, whose regular exhibitions provided the means for emergent as well as established furniture, glass, metal and other designers and craftsmen to display their ideas and products. Unlike Paris's two established annual exhibitions, held at the Grand Palais and devoted primarily to the fine arts, the yearly salon of the Société des Artistes Décorateurs was intended to give prominence to decorators. In the early years of the century and up to the 1920s, the salon continued to provide an excellent forum for new designs and model rooms. Some of its founding members, in fact, including Paul Follot, Pierre Chareau and Maurice Dufrêne, became leading lights of the Art Deco style and creators of some of its most exemplary interiors.

In 1903 another exhibition, the Salon d'Automne, was inaugurated at the Petit Palais (it later moved to the larger, more prestigious Grand Palais). Its aim was to omit no significant artist or designer, most especially those whom the official salons had ignored, and consequently some of the premier names in furniture and interior design (and, of course, painting and sculpture) were featured over the years, among them Ruhlmann, Paul Poiret's Atelier Martine, Le Corbusier and Charlotte Perriand.

These annual exhibitions, then, meant that the art and design worlds, and indeed the general public, were regularly made aware of and treated to innovative and outstanding creations by both established designers and firms and up-and-coming ones. Foreigners were also featured, such as the Deutscher Werkbund at the 1910 Salon d'Automne.

A wealth of journals, yearbooks, catalogues, design portfolios and other printed and illustrated matter enabled a wider-than-ever distribution of design ideas, both original and second-hand, not only via editorial matter, such as salon reviews, but also via advertisements taken out by design firms, such as Leleu and Dominique in France, Curtis Moffat and Betty Joel in Great Britain. Not surprisingly, France had the largest number of magazines covering new (and sometimes period) design.

Also in France there were produced, mainly in the mid to late 1920s in the wake of the 1925 exhibition, albums of high-quality, hand-coloured *pochoir* prints of interiors. In the *pochoir* process, almost as painstaking as – and therefore not entirely dissimilar to – layer-on-layer lacquering, numerous cut-out stencils (sometimes up to twenty) were used to produce multihued and minutely detailed images. Advanced photomechanical lithographic techniques were also in general use by the 1920s, enabling magazines – such as *The Studio* in Britain – to print fairly sophisticated colour illustrations (some of these, however, were inferior reproductions of original *pochoir* prints taken from French periodicals).

Originally the 1925 Paris Exposition was to have taken place in 1915, and an official committee was set up by the French Chamber of Deputies in 1912 to organize it. But it was postponed to 1916, then again – because of World War I – to 1922, then, because of lingering postwar problems, to 1924. It finally opened in April 1925, carried over from the previous year due to construction delays. Despite the intervening years from when the exhibition was initially envisaged and when it eventually came to occur, the commitment of the organizers remained firmly rooted in the present. Modernity was the theme, and a 1911 report presented by the then president of the Société des Artistes Décorateurs, René Guilleré, stated unequivocally that 'this exposition must be exclusively of Art Moderne'; he added that, 'Any copy or pastiche of past styles would not be allowed'.

After much discussion and debate, the location selected for the Exposition was the city centre. Charles Plumet was elected chief architect and Louis Bonnier was to oversee its extensive landscaping. The main gate was the Porte d'Honneur, beside the Grand Palais, and it led straight across the Seine, via the Pont Alexandre III, and down the lengthy Esplanade to the Place des Invalides. Over 130 separate exhibits – pavilions, galleries, restaurants – were scattered over the 35,000 square-metre area, surrounded by gardens, statuary, fountains, fairground rides and games.

Arguably the most elegant, if not – at least to a certain, discerning element of the population – the most popular display was that of the master *ensemblier* Emile-Jacques Ruhlmann (1879-1933). The architect of his Hôtel du Collectionneur was Pierre Patout, and its exterior features included a gate by premier *ferronnier*, or wrought-ironworker, Edgar Brandt; *La Danse*, a bas-relief by Joseph Bernard; frescoes by Henri Marret, and a freestanding stone sculpture of stylized neoclassical figures by Alfred-Auguste Janniot, entitled *A la gloire de Jean Goujon* (the French Renaissance sculptor). Inside the white-washed, stepped, essentially geometric structure were six model rooms created by Ruhlmann and Patout, featuring the finest furniture and *objets d'art* by Ruhlmann and a pantheon of top names: Georges Bastard, Emile Decoeur, François-Emile Décorchement, Jean Dunand, Léon Jallot, Pierre Legrain, Emile Lenoble, Jean Puiforcat and Henri Rapin among them.

The Eiffel Tower displayed fancy illuminated finery during the 1925 Exposition. Over 200,000 coloured bulbs created various decorative patterns on all four sides of the structure, a glittering public-relations ploy, courtesy of the Citroën company.

At the opposite end of the design spectrum from the lavish Hôtel du Collectionneur was L'Esprit Nouveau, the controversial pavilion Le Corbusier designed for the fair. Named after the magazine he and Amédée Ozenfant had started in 1920, the pavilion was begun at the eleventh hour, in April 1925, following much debate with fair organizers Plumet and Bonnier. The concrete, glass and steel structure, starkly rectilinear and somewhat sparsely – and disappointingly – furnished with mass-produced furniture, was not a straightforward embodiment of Le Corbusier's definition of a house as 'a machine for living in', but it was light, airy and reasonably inexpensive and practical as domestic structures went. Its walls were white and hung with Cubist paintings; it had a practical, split-level construction and it was sympathetic to the environment as well (being built around a tree, whose verdant upper branches blossomed out from a round opening in the house's roof).

Still, Ruhlmann's pavilion, and those of the other premier *ensembliers* and ateliers, were at the time the most popular with the fair-going public, and they – rather than the single Modernist proclamation-in-stone of Le Corbusier – have come to embody true, unadulterated Art Deco.

One of the major attractions at the 1925 fair was the Musée d'Art Contemporain, designed by the Compagnie des Arts Français, the Paris interior-decorating firm founded in 1919 as an *'entreprise collective de production artisanale'* by Louis Süe (1875-1968) and André Mare (1885-1932). Like Ruhlmann, Süe et Mare (as they were generally known) did their best to make their 'Museum of Contemporary Art' an outstanding, even over-the-top showcase of the best room settings they were capable of putting together, along with their numerous collaborators. The pavilion itself was one of a matching pair of simple, single-storey, domed structures which Süe, who had trained as an architect, designed; the other being the showcase for Maison Fontaine (a firm which had helped to finance Süe et Mare and which took over the Compagnie des Arts Français when the two principals left in 1928).

The Ambassade Française, or French Embassy, was another 'concept' pavilion of 24 model rooms in two wings, all displaying the collective talents of Paris's top designers. The massive undertaking was sponsored by the French government and presented under the auspices of the Société des Artistes Décorateurs (though the participants did not have to be members of the S.A.D.). The official, ambassadorial wing contained reception rooms and offices, while the other was the Ambassador's living quarters, with bedrooms, bathroom, music room and gymnasium; both sides had a *bureau-bibliothèque* (study-library), dining room and *fumoir* (smoking room).

Among the other rooms comprising the bipartite pavilion were a Modernist entry hall by Robert Mallet-Stevens, a smoking room and gymnasium by Francis Jourdain, an art gallery by Michel Roux-Spitz, an elegant anteroom by Paul Follot (produced in collaboration with Au Bon Marché's Pomone atelier, of which he was director), a handsome *bureau-bibliothèque* by Pierre Chareau and the Ambassador's bedroom by Georges Chevalier and Léon Jallot. Ruhlmann, Jules Leleu and dozens of others contributed designs or interiors, and the architecture and overall presentation of the pavilion were supervised by Henri Rapin and Pierre Selmersheim.

Model domestic interiors, as well as commercial displays, were designed for the fair by other noted *ensembliers*, architects, decorators, furniture and object designers, and design partnerships, whether long-established, newly formed or temporary. Premier Art Nouveau-era goldsmith René Lalique, who at the start of the twentieth century turned his designing talents chiefly to the medium of glass, designed the central motif of the Parfumerie Française display in the Grand Palais (whose overall design chief was Armand-Albert Rateau), a fountain-like glass sculpture of wide, looping arcs surmounting the radiating arms of display cases.

Another design workshop, Paul Poiret's Atelier Martine, provided the furnishings of the couturier's three barges, painted on the outside with vivid floral motifs and moored on the Left Bank of the Seine (Raoul Dufy contributed fourteen paintings of high-society pastimes – regattas, balls and horse races – to one of them).

Unlike the simple, for the most part unfussy, exteriors of the Lalique, Süe et Mare, Ruhlmann and Le Corbusier pavilions, those of the four department-store ateliers – La Maîtrise, Pomone, Primavera and Studium-Louvre – featured elaborate façades and abundant decorative and architectural details. Their interior displays were similarly lavish and variegated. Maurice Dufrêne, director of La Maîtrise, designed the interior of that atelier's pavilion, along with the building's trio of architects, Georges Beau, Joseph Hiriart and Georges Tribout. Besides the main exhibition gallery, five model rooms were contained inside: a bedroom for a gentleman, a living room, a dining room, a study-library and a lady's boudoir; the latter, by Suzanne Guiguichon and Gabriel Englinger, was highly evocative of the Louis-Philippe style. Two upper-level tearooms surrounded additional display cases featuring objects produced by La Maîtrise. Pomone's interior, designed by its director, Paul Follot, also contained room settings in addition to display areas. An entrance hall, study, smoking room, dining room and lady's boudoir were located on the ground floor, and upstairs there were two bedrooms.

The exterior of Primavera's pavilion was the most dramatic of the four, comprising a circular lower section surmounted by a dome. The interior featured works by Louis Sognot, Claude Lévy, Marcel Guillemard, Jean Burkhalter and Charlotte Chauchet-Guilleré, the latter the director of Primavera, which had been founded by her husband, René Guilleré. She

The Paris salons were among the various forums where designers could display their talents. The 1914 catalogue of the ninth Salon of the Société des Artistes Décorateurs has a striking cover designed by François-Louis Schmied. Its chequerboard border shows a Viennese influence, but its central floral motif looks forward to French *art moderne* in full bloom.

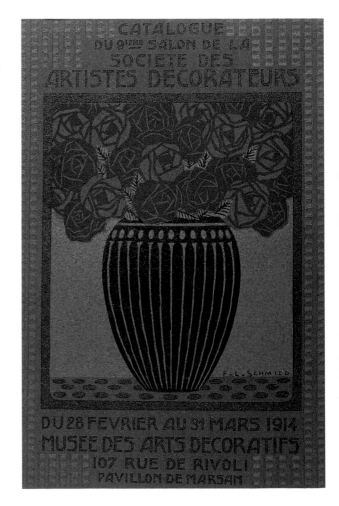

The 1925 Exposition was the subject of a wealth of promotional and critical material. This prospectus puts equal emphasis on the artistic, industrial and international aspects of the fair, with its representations of a palette, measuring device and globe.

designed a bedroom in the pavilion whose veneered furniture was simple, well-made and sombre-toned. Studium-Louvre's pavilion, an octagonal edifice distinguished by eight stone urns carved with flowers and set amid real plants on the first-storey outdoor terrace, was designed by André Fréchet, Maurice Matet and Studium's director, Etienne Kohlmann. A living room and boudoir, created by Fréchet along with Pierre Lahalle and Georges Lavard, were markedly traditional in style, with richly veneered furniture.

In other countries besides France, of course, a wide variety of exhibitions were organized which featured model interiors, or elements of modern design in a simple display setting. In the United States, in fact, a travelling loan exhibition to eight museums was presented at the Metropolitan Museum of Art in New York in 1926, the year after the Paris fair, and featured some 400 objects lent in the main by the designers themselves. There was even a modern French-style room installation presented in the autumn of 1925 at F. Schumacher and Co., the New York textile manufacturer, featuring works by Edgar Brandt, René Lalique and Paul Follot. Two significant showcases for European designers were shows organized by the Manhattan department stores, Lord & Taylor and R.H. Macy. The latter's Art-in-Trade Exposition took place in spring 1927 and was in part the work of the Metropolitan Museum's President, Robert W. de Forest, who stated that, 'Much as I am interested in bringing art to the museum, I am more interested in bringing good art into the home'. Top American designers were included and Paul T. Frankl contributed a complete room setting dominated by his skyscraper furniture. The massive early 1928 Lord & Taylor show, An Exposition of Modern French Decorative Art, showcased nearly 500 works by Süe et Mare, Ruhlmann, Dunand and over twenty others, including the painters Picasso, Braque and Utrillo.

New York's Metropolitan Museum was arguably the strongest exponent of modern design. Besides being one of the venues for A Selected Collection of Modern Decorative and Industrial Art in 1926, the museum sponsored the hugely successful 1929 show (its eleventh such annual design exhibit), The Architect and the Industrial Arts, with room settings by eight architects, including Raymond Hood, Eliel Saarinen, Eugene Schoen and Joseph Urban, and objects by some 150 designers, craftsmen and companies, as well as the 1934 show of Contemporary American Industrial Art.

By the 1930s, many institutions and associations, both new and old, had jumped on the bandwagon: the American Union of Decorative Artists and Craftsmen (AUDAC) held two annual shows, the first in 1930 at the Grand Central Palace in New York, the second a year later at the Brooklyn Museum. The American Designers' Gallery, Inc., had its first show in 1928; this organization was formed to promote works by Donald Deskey, Paul Frankl,

Wolfgang and Pola Hoffmann, Ruth Reeves and others, but, unfortunately, as with other such endeavours, the Depression caused its quick demise. Such was the fate of Contempora, Inc., as well, which was made up of European designers – among them Paul Poiret and the German Bruno Paul – and staged only one exhibit in New York, of modern 'harmonized' rooms.

Mention should be made of the three major world's fairs held in the United States as well, although these did not prove influential to interior design in the way of the 1925 Paris Exposition. More forays into the future and escapist fun fairs than showcases for art and design, Chicago's Century of Progress Exhibition (1933-34), the New York World's Fair (1939-40) and San Francisco's Golden Gate International Exposition (1939) featured outstanding architecture, murals, sculpture and technological displays, but on the whole they were showplaces for industrial design and designers, not for interior design (although room settings by Paul T. Frankl, Kem Weber, Gilbert Rohde and Marcel Breuer were featured at the California fair). There were two other significant international exhibitions in Paris, the 1931 Exposition Coloniale Internationale and the 1937 Exposition Internationale des Arts et Techniques.

Elsewhere in Europe, regular and one-off exhibitions were sponsored, featuring both domestic and international designs. Among many others, there were the Stuttgart Weissenhofsiedlung (1927), the Stockholm Exhibition (1930) and the Exposition Internationale et Universelle in Brussels (1935). The latter included among its displays exhibits by the Parisian Société des Artistes Décorateurs and the Union des Artistes Modernes, the latter of which had been formed in 1930 as a functionalist reaction against and antidote to the overdone, over-decorative designs that had dominated the 1925 fair.

In Britain, various design groups, trade shows and more ambitious exhibitions featured the works of resident designers, and occasionally Continental designs were displayed (a show of Alvar Aalto's work at Fortnum & Mason and an exhibition of D.I.M.'s furnishings at Shoolbred, the decorators, in 1928 among them). There was the 1924 British Empire Exhibition at Wembley, the 1933 and 1934 Dorland Hall exhibitions of British Industrial Art (the next, British Art in Industry, was held in 1935 at Burlington House), the 1934 exhibition, Contemporary Industrial Art in the Home, the Women's Fair at Olympia (1938), the British Empire Exhibition in Glasgow (1938) and, of course, the ongoing *Daily Mail* Ideal Home Exhibitions, which had been inaugurated in 1908. Associations of designers, like the MARS (Modern Architectural Research Group), sponsored exhibitions as well (MARS's first, at the New Burlington Galleries, opened in January 1938). The premier names in modern British architecture and interior and industrial design were associated with MARS, including Wells Coates, Raymond McGrath, Serge Chermayeff, Berthold Lubetkin and E. Maxwell Fry.

Lord & Taylor was one of several New York department stores to jump on the *art moderne* bandwagon. In 1927 they displayed this interior, with its French-style chairs, skyscraper bookcase and doors painted with cheerful naïve motifs; the furniture and doors were yellow, red and green.

At the 1921 Salon d'Automne René Herbst, whose later interiors were strongly Modernist and devoid of decoration, presented a striking ensemble (*above*), with nicely curving and geometric forms and dense patterns of stylized blossoms filling the silk-covered walls, screen and upholstery. A lesser known designer, Léridon, created the flower-, pillow- and fur-strewn space (*left*) for the same salon. The amaranth, burr amboyna and marble *chiffonier* is quite handsome, but the rest of the setting borders on period kitsch.

GREAT EXHIBITIONS

Exhibited at the 1925 Paris Exposition was this studio (*right*) conceived by Lucie Renaudot. The furniture, largely veneered in Macassar ebony, was made by the firm of P.A. Dumas, and the metal vases are by Dunand.

Rouen painter Raymond Quibel designed the dining room (*below*), exhibited at the 1925 Paris fair by Saddier et Fils, a French furniture-making firm that began producing Moderne ensembles in the 1920s. Lalique provided the room's glassware, Puiforcat its silver and the furniture is of exotic palissander.

The refined elegance of a Ruhlmann interior is seen in the bedroom in his Hôtel du Collectionneur (*above*). Its walls were hung with ivory damask, the dressing table (on the right) was veneered in amboyna, its top inlaid with shagreen and ivory, and the wall lamp has a fan-shaped shade of alabaster.

The round boudoir (*left*) in Ruhlmann's pavilion is somewhat fancifully rendered in this representation (and erroneously coloured – the actual room was executed in green, white and gold), but *faux* shades aside, it is a delicate, highly feminine space, with its Macassar ebony and ivory rolltop desk, handsome appliques and stylized floral basket above the white marble fireplace.

Ruhlmann's Grand Salon (*left*) was dedicated to music and featured a Gaveau grand piano, veneered, like most of the room's furniture, in Macassar ebony. An unabashed display of opulence, the room included richly patterned, silk-covered walls; a glittering chandelier with matching wall lights; a massive cabinet lacquered black by Dunand (with an animal motif by Lambert-Rucki), and *Les Perruches*, a painting by Jean Dupas. A. Rigal's monumental mural on the domed ceiling (*below left*) illustrated Beethoven's symphonies.

The partnership of Süe et Mare created the Musée d'Art Contemporain at the 1925 fair, whose Rotonde is seen here (*below*). Presided over by a huge chandelier set amid gilded festoons and garlands, the room featured a Pleyel piano and ebony and ormolu desk, both supported on massive alate legs – an exaggerated device often used by Süe et Mare and derived from eighteenth-century French furniture. The gilt-wood chairs and ottoman are upholstered after Charles Dufresne's design.

The talents of René Lalique were much in demand at the 1925 Paris Exposition. Not only did he have his own pavilion, but he also contributed to the Parfumerie Française display in the Grand Palais, where his fountain-like glass sculpture (*left*) surmounted the display cases, as well as creating a dining room (*above*) for the Sèvres pavilion. The room's marble walls were incised and silvered with a lush forest scene complete with wild-boar hunt; a palissander and glass table was set with Lalique glass and Sèvres porcelain, and a grid of Modernist light fittings was affixed to the ceiling.

37

GREAT EXHIBITIONS

The Ambassade Francaise pavilion included two *fumoirs* (smoking rooms). The one by Jean Dunand was ruled by a lacquered, exotic richness, but Francis Jourdain's *fumoir* (*right*) was a twentieth-century symphony of geometry, simplicity, spaciousness and colour. It well illustrates Jourdain's statement that 'a room could be very luxuriously fitted out if we empty rather than fill it with furniture'.

Henri Rapin designed the elegant salon (*below*) for the Ambassade Francaise pavilion. The collective talents of Paris's top designers came together in this imaginary 'French Embassy', which comprised 24 model rooms in two wings, one intended for official business, the other a private residence.

Handsome kitchens, like the one (*left*) created by René Gabriel, with furnishings by Etablissements Harmand, also featured in the fair. In actuality, the chequerboard design on the floor – a nod to Secession Vienna – was much more tightly composed, but otherwise the green- and white-painted furniture and mouldings and the uniform rectilinearity of the space made for a crisp and cheerful effect. On the other hand, the kitchen created by André Groult and produced by Les Constructeurs associés de Paris (*below left*), is far more curvilinear and elegant, from the large curved and small circular windows to the continuous blue loop motif along the wall. It is also a more traditional, utilitarian space, with its extensive cupboards and gleaming copper pots.

Among the bathrooms on view at the Exposition was a handsome and spacious marble-sheathed model (*below*) by Marcel Dalmas. The octagonal window under the angled arch nicely complements the mirror surmounting the console table with metal-tendrilled base.

Britain's Ideal Home Exhibition, inaugurated in 1908, provided an annual venue for designers and firms to display their Moderne as well as traditional products. The dining and sitting room ensemble (*above*), with its plump easy chairs, target-like area rug and elegantly curved desk and cabinet, was in the 1935 show; it was presented by Bowman Brothers of Camden Town.

In the United States, various *art moderne*-minded retail stores and galleries, mainly in the big cities, offered contemporary furniture and objects to an eager, urbane clientele. This assortment of metal and glass pieces (*left*) includes a steel lamp by Donald Deskey and copper bookends by Walter von Nessen (made by the Chase Brass & Copper Company).

New York's Metropolitan Museum was a significant force behind the promotion of Art Deco furniture, objects and interiors, both foreign and domestic. The landmark exhibition, The Architect and the Industrial Arts, presented to great acclaim in 1929, featured the works of important architect-designers working in America. Eliel Saarinen's dining room (*above*) is a symphony of subtle diamond and triangle patterns covering floor, walls, mantelpiece and other furnishings. Joseph Urban created the man's den (*right*) with its profusion of geometric motifs, smart nesting tables and bright splash of colours making up the area rug; it is a practical, cheerful space, a world apart from the usual stodgy, leather-covered study. Raymond Hood's executive office (*top*) is likewise a bright, pleasant, decidedly Moderne workspace, with its floral-embellished windows, vertical blinds, aluminium-framed furniture and smart lighting fixtures.

The **Musée des Arts Africains et Océaniens** in Paris was built by the architects Laprade and Jaussely for the 1931 Exposition Coloniale; its two salons, one furnished by Ruhlmann (*opposite*), the other by Eugène Printz (*left*), were connected by a gallery. In Ruhlmann's room (later the office of Marshal Hubert Lyautey) can be seen a quartet of the master's plump 'Eléphant' chairs, as well as a desk of Macassar ebony and shagreen, and massive metal vases by Edgar Brandt. On the wall is a fresco by Louis Bouquet depicting the cultural contributions made by Africa. A detail of Printz's double-tiered desk, one of two in the room is on the left of the photograph (*left*); the tapestry-covered chair features on its back a French cockerel perching on a palm tree below which stand a camel and an elephant.

The Contemporary American Industrial Art show of 1934 was another significant display of modern design at New York's Metropolitan Museum. Two of its most sparkling, up-to-date interiors were created by well-known designers who worked in a variety of media. Donald Deskey's dining room (*above*) featured a wall of shimmering glass bricks lit from behind, a burr redwood and frosted-glass table (with a light sandwiched between base and top) and smart chairs made partly of Metallon, a brand-new nickel-silver material). The streamlined mock-up of an industrial designer's office (*opposite*), designed by Raymond Loewy with Lee Simonson, offered an efficient, harmonious and thoroughly modern working environment.

Armand-Albert Rateau created for Jeanne Lanvin a lovely, though somewhat traditional boudoir, when he designed her Paris flat in 1920-22.

CHAPTER 3
FRENCH INTERIORS
THE PARIS ENSEMBLIERS

The seeds of Art Deco were sown as early as 1901, when a group of French designers – among them Hector Guimard, Eugène Grasset, Raoul Lachenal and Eugène Gaillard, stalwarts of Art Nouveau, and Paul Follot, Maurice Dufrêne and Emile Decoeur, young designers who were to become leading lights of Art Deco – joined together to form the Société des Artistes Décorateurs. Their intent was to organize an exhibition of forward-looking, modern decorative art – not established design, the way the 1900 Exposition Universelle had featured waning Art Nouveau. Alas, the planned exhibition did not come about for two decades – the 1925 Exposition Internationale des Arts Décoratifs et Industriels Modernes – but examples of the contemporary design that was to be known much later as Art Deco appeared considerably earlier, in individual objects and room settings alike, at salon exhibitions and in actual interiors.

The concept, indeed the profession, of *ensemblier* and the total room *ensemble* had become part of the Paris design vocabulary and repertoire by 1911, partly encouraged by the phenomenal success of the German applied arts display at the 1910 Salon d'Automne. The Deutscher Werkbund settings, such as the dining room by Adalbert Niemeyer and the lady's bedroom by Karl Bertsch, impressed the Paris designers, perhaps not so much in terms of overall workmanship and forms as in their stylistic harmony and even their colours. Indeed, the palette of the *ensembliers* at this time was influenced not only by the rich, vibrant hues of the Ballets Russes, but also by the darker shades – browns, purples, black – characteristic of the Werkbund. They also favoured painted wood, exotic lacquer and inlays of rare wood and materials such as ivory, mother-of-pearl and silver. Often the early Art Deco *ensemblier* employed at least a vestigial curve and a trace of decoration, but clean-cut, purely rectilinear forms (these showing a German or Austrian influence) were certainly present in their designs.

The creators of the modern interior in Paris were individuals, partnerships, established and long-lived design firms, and – a novelty – the all-in-one workshop-cum-designer service provided by the four *grands magasins* of Paris. The latter represented a totally new concept: to go to a major retail establishment to fill all one's design needs, and it proved to be a highly successful one. The interiors of the premier Parisian designers and firms, as well as those of the four department-store design studios, came to embody high-style Art Deco, as well as influence its progenitors throughout Europe and the world. Yet, the Modernist trend exemplified by Le Corbusier, Charlotte Perriand, Djo-Bourgeois, Pierre Chareau, Eileen Gray and Robert Mallet-Stevens cannot be ignored, since it also greatly influenced subsequent design – in retrospect, even more so than Parisian Art Deco *de luxe* – and, besides, the designs of this group were not all severe, unadorned rectilinearity: strong decorative elements asserted themselves, along with no-nonsense tubular steel, leather upholstery and white walls.

Soon after 1912, Paul Poiret (1879-1944) – already under the sensuous, colourful influence of the Ballets Russes in his fashions – was displaying interiors marked by a sophisticated unity and harmony of design, such as the tastefully decorated shop interior which his Atelier Martine, established in 1912, designed for the purpose of selling Poiret's line of perfumes, Rosine. Other more typical Atelier Martine room settings, with their bright colours, spontaneous designs and plush, cosy atmospheres, were indeed, as one contemporary source stated, 'capable of propagating a new mode of decoration and furnishing'.

Arguably the most significant event in 1912 affecting the future of Art Deco involved another couturier, in fact Poiret's former employer, Jacques Doucet (1853-1929), but in his guise as an eminent collector, not as influential fashion designer. In the years preceding 1912, Doucet had accumulated a superb collection of Old Master paintings and drawings, rare books, and eighteenth-century French furniture and objects, but in that year he proceeded to dispose of nearly his entire collection (not the antiquarian volumes), which fetched some thirteen million francs at auction. He decided to give up his home on the rue Spontini which had housed that impressive collection, to embark on new areas of collecting and to furnish his new residence, at 46 avenue du Bois, with modern fine and decorative arts – in essence, a symbolic purge of the past. He enlisted Paul Iribe (1883-1935), a friend of Poiret, to supervise the design of his new apartment, and Iribe's assistant, Pierre Legrain (1889-1929), was put in charge of its decoration.

Doucet's apartment, when it was completed, was called a 'temple of Modern Art' by one critic, and in that temple a pantheon of designers and artists displayed their talents, in without doubt the most outstanding example of a modern interior at that time. Unfortunately, few people saw the inside of that residence, and more are familiar with the studio on the rue Saint-James in Neuilly, to which Doucet had moved in 1929 (also the year of his death). Many of the same pieces appeared in the studio, and Legrain was responsible for its decoration. Among the noted designers whose works graced Doucet's abodes were Eileen Gray, Marcel Coard, Pierre Chareau, Jean Lurçat, Gustave Miklos, René Lalique, Pierre Legrain, Rose Adler and Jean Dunand. Doucet was above all a collector and connoisseur, and his personal tastes were made very evident in all his rooms, with a great deal of help from Legrain, who was to work extensively for his client until both their deaths in 1929 (Iribe had in fact left Paris in 1914 for the United States).

A colour photograph of one room of the Neuilly studio provides an excellent glimpse into the life of this most discerning of collectors. A massive rosewood, leather and ivory sofa by Marcel Coard – the wood deftly carved to imitate the weave of tropical rattan – is strewn with animal skins; over it hangs Douanier Rousseau's masterwork, *The Snake Charmer*. On the floor are area carpets by Jean Lurçat and Eileen Gray's black- and silver-lacquered round table, its legs carved in the manner of African sculpture. An African-inspired stool by Legrain stands aside a pair of moulded-glass doors by Lalique featuring male athletes in motion, and a chest by Iribe is also on view. Superb paintings and sculptures covered the walls and flat surfaces, and although many of the objects Doucet commissioned were outstanding masterpieces in their own right – such as Rose Adler's ebony side table covered with a cityscape motif made of sharkskin, Eileen Gray's red-lacquered screen *Le Destin* with nude classical figures in dark blue outlined with silver, and the red-lacquered file cabinet by Legrain and Dunand – they comfortably coexisted alongside the fine art, at the same time holding their own and making subtle design statements. Doucet loved objects made of rich, exotic materials – sharkskin, rock crystal, ivory, lacquerwork – and, together with fur throws, they made a fine setting for his African, antique and Oriental objects.

The master *ensemblier* of the period, however, was Emile-Jacques Ruhlmann. His love of fine, luxurious materials, the innate elegance and refinement of his pieces (so reminiscent of eighteenth-century France) and his immense commercial success are undeniable. And though the age of elegance was all but finished by the end of the 1925 Exposition, at which he was arguably the brightest star, he was not afraid to move with the times and to tone down his style, making it subtler and more angular, even including distinctly Moderne elements, such as chromed-metal drawer pulls and swivel chairs.

The son of an affluent builder, Ruhlmann started working for his father as a teenager, taking over the family business in 1907, upon the elder Ruhlmann's death. Throughout his early years, working on building sites and dealing with contractors, he longed for a career as a designer. A keen sketcher whose renderings of furniture filled dozens of notebooks, Ruhlmann himself was not a cabinet-maker, but by 1913 his firm was exhibiting pieces of furniture, albeit ones he had made elsewhere (he subcontracted his furniture until 1923): a Macassar ebony *bergère* inlaid with ivory dots was shown at the Salon d'Automne and promptly purchased by Jacques Doucet. The Ruhlmann empire was now firmly divided into two: the wallpaper, paint and mirror-work atelier he had inherited at one address, 10 rue de Maleville, his newly established interior-design and furnishing firm at another, 27 rue de Lisbonne. The war years were relatively uneventful for Ruhlmann, but in 1919 a company, Ruhlmann et Laurent, was set up with friend and decorating contractor, Pierre Laurent, an enterprise which would allow him to oversee the interior-design firm, and Laurent to run the hugely successful house-restoration and painting arm at rue de Maleville. By 1927, besides his rue de Lisbonne interior-design premises, where the selling and designing were done (and where he had his own office), he had transformed his rue d'Ouessant address (acquired in 1919 for the purpose of accommodating the paint, upholstery, mirror and wallpaper departments) into a garage and paint store (ground floor), a lacquering shop (first floor), an upholstery shop (second floor), a cabinet-making shop (called 'Atelier A' from 1928) on the third storey, 'Atelier B' on the fourth and a panelling workshop on the fifth.

The number of interior-design commissions received by Ruhlmann over his career (upon his death his trusted associate and nephew, Alfred Porteneuve, was responsible for finishing outstanding commissions and liquidating the stock, Laurent keeping his part of the firm in rue de Maleville), coupled with his triumphs at the 1925 Exposition and various salons and exhibitions, are an impressive testimony to his greatness. Couturiers, manufacturers, *parfumeurs*, architects, bankers, museum officials, industrialists, writers, even an Eastern potentate, the Maharajah of Indore, numbered among his clients, and he provided furnishings and interiors for ocean liners, restaurants, civic buildings, even a cinema and stage set. Each room setting, whether real or artificial, usually bore several unmistakable Ruhlmann touches: expertly veneered and exquisitely ivory-inlaid furniture; elegant mirrors and lighting fixtures; subtle, decorative details, such as tassels on drawer pulls and bolster pillows; beautifully patterned upholstery, wall-coverings and carpets; handsome forms appropriate to their setting, be it a delicate lady's desk on slim, *sabot*-footed legs or a massive fantail-top executive desk, with strategically situated pigeonholes, bellpush and wastepaper basket.

Louis Süe (1875-1968) and André Mare (1885-1932) founded La Compagnie des Arts Français in 1919, remaining with it until 1928 (when it was taken over by Jacques Adnet, who ran it until 1959). In their desire to combat an individualism they deemed undesirable in interior design, they gathered together the talents of some of Paris's top artists, designers and craftsmen, each of whom could participate in the communal enterprise. Among those who made contributions were the glassmaker Marinot, the sculptors Despiau and Maillol, the ironworker Richard Desvallières and the painters Paul Véra, Marie Laurencin and Gustave Jaulmes. Their best-known collaborative effort was the Musée d'Art Contemporain at the 1925 Paris fair, but several other notable interiors, including couturier Jean Patou's home, the French Embassy in Warsaw and the Grand Salon of the liner *Ile-de-France*, were created in the nine short years that the Compagnie des Arts Français existed under their direction.

Despite their own highly pronounced preference for collective work on all their projects, it was the distinctive designs of Süe et Mare themselves that gave their interiors most of their appeal. Many of their forms and details harked back to Louis Quinze and Louis Seize designs, and their own addition of modern, stylized elements – outsized scrolls, flowers or wings – made them uniquely their own. Süe et Mare designs have been referred to as 'exhibition pieces', and indeed they had a theatrical flair to them, unlike the quiet subtlety of much of the *oeuvre* of Ruhlmann, who oversaw the production of his pieces and was altogether more critical of how they were produced.

The most renowned of Süe's solo commissions came from cosmetics queen Helena Rubinstein, the interior of whose seventeenth-century Parisian house he renovated around 1938. Süe's task was more to design a complementary setting for his client's extensive, eclectic collection of art and objects than to play his earlier role of *ensemblier*, and no doubt Rubinstein herself guided him with a firm hand. Some of the resultant rooms were well-balanced, tasteful and modern, but others were baroque extravaganzas.

Another design group of note in Paris was D.I.M. (Décoration Intérieure Moderne) which, like the Compagnie des Arts Français of Süe et Mare, was often known by the surnames of two of its designers, René Joubert (d. 1931) and Philippe Petit (d. 1945). Actually, D.I.M. had been founded after World War I by Joubert and theatrical designer Georges Mouveau, whom Petit replaced in 1924. Set up to make furniture as well as create interiors, D.I.M. forswore the overblown decorative elements of Süe et Mare and were drawn more towards the subtlety of Ruhlmann, though their handsomely veneered pieces were generally imbued with their own down-to-earth solidity and sense of geometry.

In 1922, the interior-design partnership of André Domin (1883-1962) and Marcel Genevrière (1885-1967) was formed, calling itself by the single name, Dominique. An early commission was to design and furnish silversmith Jean Puiforcat's home at Biarritz, and they also furnished the Houbigant perfume factory at Neuilly. In 1926 they, along with Puiforcat, Chareau, Legrain and jeweller Raymond Templier, formed the 'Groupe des Cinq', and they exhibited regularly at the Galerie Barbazanges. Dominique's furniture and interiors were made of the most elegant materials – amaranth, ebony and palissander, often covered with shagreen or parchment – but their forms, especially after the 1925 fair, in which they participated, were on the whole more Cubist and geometric, less subtle and gently curved than those of Ruhlmann (though no less elegant).

A designer who, much like Ruhlmann, remained a singular, almost solitary, force in 1920s design was Armand-Albert Rateau (1882-1938). Unlike Ruhlmann, however, Rateau possessed an unusual, one might even say obsessive and eccentric, personal vision, one devoted to antiquity and consequently based on the use of bronze, that most ancient of materials. He was a student of

La Compagnie des Arts Français, the design firm of Louis Süe and André Mare, created this dining room *c.* 1925. Paper with an updated *déjeuner sur l'herbe* motif – painted by André Marty and produced by Zuber – covers the walls, while the area carpet and gondole-type chairs are adorned with dense floral patterns.

drawing and wood-carving at the acclaimed Ecole Boulle in Paris, and worked for several interior-decoration firms before being named manager of the Maison Alavoine in 1905. After the war he set up on his own, and his output was heavily reminiscent of the furniture and objects he saw in 1914 while visiting Pompeii and the museum at Naples, with Syrian, Persian and other exotic touches. Rateau rarely exhibited his pieces publicly, content and successful with his commissions from a wealthy, discerning clientele. Most of these came from the couturière, Jeanne Lanvin, whose private house and fashion salon he designed and furnished (he also managed an interior-design firm that was part of Lanvin's empire), and for whom he spectacularly – mostly in shades of gold and cornflower and lapis-lazuli blue – decorated the Théâtre Daunou in Paris in the early 1920s.

Another Parisian decorator known for his metalwork was Jean Dunand (1877-1942), though he was equally acclaimed for his lacquered furniture as well as for his model-room interiors combining both these elements. Geneva-born Dunand trained as a sculptor, turning to metalwork around 1903 and lacquer a decade or so later. His best-known interior was the smoking room in the Ambassade Française at the 1925 Paris fair, but he collaborated with other designers, such as Ruhlmann, creating several rooms full of lacquered furniture for Madeleine Vionnet (the dress designer who invented the bias cut) and exhibited as well at other international fairs, including an ensemble of lacquered furniture at the 1939-40 New York World's Fair.

André Groult (1884-1967), who was married to Paul Poiret's sister, Nicole (a close friend of decorative painter Marie Laurencin, whose canvases he often featured in his interiors), was a thoughtful decorator often inspired by classical French design. Although he was equally talented and comfortable with creating a masculine room sensitive to a man's needs and tastes, he is probably best remembered for his pale-toned, quite obviously feminine rooms, with their sharkskin-covered beds, cabinets and chairs standing on delicate, tapering legs, and carpets, paintings and other elements often in pastel tones.

Another exponent of the opulent school of Art Deco was Jules Leleu (1883-1961), a sculptor-turned-interior decorator, whose furniture and interiors have been compared to those of Groult, Süc et Mare and Ruhlmann. A traditionalist (as opposed to Modernist), Leleu was inspired by French eighteenth-century forms and taste. He supplied several model rooms at the 1925 Paris fair with his pieces, as well as displaying a living-room ensemble at his own Esplanade des Invalides space. He also showed at many salons, provided designs for several ocean liners and designed rooms for numerous French embassies (including those in Brazil, Japan, Poland and Turkey). Following in Leleu's wake was André Arbus (1903-1969), who learned the art of *ébénisterie* in the workshop of his father and grandfather in Toulouse,

Jean Dunand, although most renowned for his metal- and lacquerwork, also created whole interiors, such as this boudoir of *c.* 1930. The curvilinear furniture forms differ from his earlier, boxy shapes, but the floral and avian scene on the far wall and the female figure seen on a panel towards the left are clear indications of his unwavering love of Oriental-inspired exotica.

This room, created by Léon Jallot, has a refined sense of geometry. The substantial marble-topped console tables, cabinet and pedestal table in this *c.* 1927 dining room are veneered in palissander.

displayed veneered furniture to much acclaim at the 1925 Exposition and finally settled in Paris in the early 1930s, where he opened a gallery, L'Epoque.

Although primarily an architect and designer of objects – wallpaper, fabrics, jewellery – Eric Bagge (1890-1978) also designed furniture and provided numerous designs, including a boudoir and bathroom in the French Embassy pavilion, for the 1925 Paris Exposition. His style began in the opulent Art Deco vein – veneered furniture encrusted with ivory and decorated with floral baskets – but later interiors were markedly more geometric, such as the living room he created for the *Ile-de-France* in 1927.

Numerous other interior designers were creating room settings in the 1920s that can be attributed to the 'decorative' school of Art Deco. Among these were Georges de Bardyère (d.1942); Louis Doumergue; Gabriel Englinger (b.1898), long connected to La Maîtrise of the Galeries Lafayette; René Gabriel (1890-1950); André Fréchet (1875-1973), long-time director of the Ecole Boulle; Suzanne Guiguichon (b.1900), who collaborated with Englinger on Louis-Philippe-style interiors; René Herbst (1891-1982), whose decorative style all but disappeared after 1925, and who became a leading Modernist and founder of the Union des Artistes Modernes; Léon Jallot (1874-1967) and his son, Maurice (b.1900), both of whom contributed to the 1925 Paris fair, but whose creations by the late 1920s came to use metal and synthetic substances; Pierre Lahalle (1877-1956); Fernand Nathan, whose creations at times echoed Restauration, Louis-Philippe, Chippendale and other sources; Henri Rapin (1873-1939), once a student of the painter Gérôme, latterly the artistic director of the Sèvres porcelain manufactory and a designer of eclectic interiors ranging from Louis Seize to coolly Modernist; Michel Roux-Spitz (1888-1957), and Tony Selmersheim (1871-1971).

One designer who effectively straddled the opulent and Modernist strains of Art Deco was Eugène Printz (1889-1948). A *maître ébéniste*, lover of wood and user of modern metals, he was able to combine within his *oeuvre* the (seemingly antithetical) luxury of veneered furniture with the simplicity and regularity of Modernist forms. He was to collaborate with the premier *maître ébéniste*, Ruhlmann, on a pavilion at the 1931 Exposition Coloniale.

Besides the interiors by *ensembliers* such as Ruhlmann, Süe et Mare and others, those room settings created for exhibitions and actual clients by the interior-decorating and workshop arms of the *grands magasins* of Paris helped heighten and spread interest in Art Deco throughout France and even elsewhere in Europe and America. Some of the individuals who worked for the Paris stores – Maurice Dufrêne and Paul Follot foremost among them – were also considered premier contemporary designers, even influential tastemakers, whose styles came to be intertwined with the establishments to which they were attached.

The first of the *grands magasins* to establish a studio was Le Printemps, whose Atelier Primavera was set up in 1913 by René Guilleré, founding member of the Société des Artistes Décorateurs (he was its president in 1911). His wife, Charlotte Chauchet-Guilleré, was selected to manage it. Besides producing furniture, the design studio created metalwork, ceramics, fabric and wallpaper. Stone- and earthenware articles were made by the Longwy pottery in Meurthe-et-Moselle, as well as at a pottery in Sainte-Radegonde, near Tours. Furniture and ironwork were constructed in Montreuil. Primavera's interiors were highly praised, and those of *directrice* Mme Chauchet-Guilleré were often singled out. Although ensembles occasionally included decorative, high-style Art Deco touches (especially early ones, such as Théodore Lambert's 1913 boudoir with its *boiserie*, silk-covered walls and gilt-lacquered surfaces), on the whole they tended to take their lead more from the straightforward, unembellished rectilinear forms of Cubism than from those of traditional styles and motifs. The interiors of Louis Sognot (1892-1970) were especially Moderne, making liberal use of chromed metal and rigid geometric forms (but not deleting fine woods from his vocabulary, as in a lovely satinwood sideboard of c. 1926).

Claude Lévy (1895-1942) was another talented individual long attached to Primavera, for which she initially created designs for dinnerware, earthenware vessels and glazed animal figures. By 1930, she had advanced to furniture and interior designs, and her first room setting was unveiled at the inaugural exhibition of the Union des Artistes Modernes. Possessing a Modernist vision, but not afraid to use high-quality woods for her veneered surfaces, Lévy produced the types of interiors that would be highly acclaimed in – and appropriate for – the fashionable American residences furnished by Kem Weber, Donald Deskey and Gilbert Rohde. She collaborated with Chareau, Francis Jourdain and Le Corbusier on furnishing the offices of the newspaper, *La Semaine à Paris*.

Marcel Guillemard (1886-1932) joined Primavera at the same time as Sognot; both had previously worked for the furniture maker, Krieger. From 1918 to 1929 he headed the design and decoration office, and was also responsible for many of the window displays. Throughout his tenure at the atelier, his style slowly but remarkably evolved, classical interiors recalling elements of eighteenth- and nineteenth-century design, giving way by the late 1920s to starkly Moderne tubular-steel furniture and Cubist-inspired forms. There was no such duality in the interiors of Jean Burkhalter (b. 1895), who collaborated with Chareau and Mallet-Stevens in addition to providing designs for Primavera. A multitalented painter, sculptor and architect, Burkhalter addressed his skills to designing metalwork, fabric, carpets and posters, and his furniture was largely of metal and eminently functional.

The other three department-store ateliers were not set up until after the war, La Maîtrise being the first in 1921. It was attached to the Galeries Lafayette, and Maurice Dufrêne (1876-1955) was named its director, a position he held for over twenty years. A founding member of the Société des Artistes Décorateurs in 1901, Dufrêne had added the design of interiors to his varied repertoire as early as 1899, when he worked for Julius Meier-Graefe's La Maison Moderne, the Art Nouveau gallery. Despite his exposure to the undulating lines of Art Nouveau, Dufrêne used the curve, as well as ornamentation, quite sparingly, certainly compared to the exuberant designs of his contemporaries. He preferred plain, solid, largely undecorated shapes for his furniture, although within his varied and long-lasting career, his eclecticism – at times comprising highly contrasting interior styles – stood out above all.

Other designers worked extensively, though not exclusively, for La Maîtrise, including Jean and Jacques Adnet, Eric Bagge, Gabriel Englinger, Suzanne Guiguichon, Pierre-Paul Montagnac and Fernand Nathan. Jacques Adnet (b. 1900) referred to himself as both an 'innovator and a classicist, champion of a tradition advancing forward'. He participated in many salons and exhibitions and had numerous interior-design commissions, including the home of American financier Frank Jay Gould, the office of the French President and several cruise ships. Although his interiors in the 1920s – on most of these he collaborated with his twin, Jean – generally comprised elegant, rectilinear furnishings of equally fine woods, sometimes embellished with parchment or even sharkskin, his increasingly minimalist 1930s furniture and interiors made use of glass and chromed metal.

Gabriel Englinger (b. 1898) and Suzanne Guiguichon (b. 1900) joined La Maîtrise in 1922 and 1921 respectively, and together they created a stunning living room in rosewood and palissander for the Maîtrise pavilion at the 1925 Paris fair. Guiguichon's style retained an element of classicism throughout her career, although later interiors were marked by straight lines, simple volumes and minimal decoration. Marseilles-born Fernand Nathan was another eclectic designer whose interiors at times reflected features of Louis Seize, Louis-Philippe, even Chippendale or other period styles. He exhibited as early as 1913 at the Salon des Artistes Décorateurs – his dining room there was described as 'referring to the Middle Ages without being a pastiche'.

Pomone, founded in 1922 as the atelier of the department store Au Bon Marché, was headed by Paul Follot (1877-1941), a designer, like Dufrêne, whose early career began in the late Art Nouveau period. He worked for Meier-Graefe's La Maison Moderne and was a founding member of the Société des Artistes Décorateurs, also like Dufrêne. He showed regularly at the salons and exhibitions, as well as designing the bulk of Pomone's pavilion at the 1925 fair and an antechamber in the Ambassade Française (also for

Pomone). Many of his interiors contained elements recalling traditional French design, his high Art Deco pieces tending to stylize those rich floral motifs he first used on his simple, elegant furniture in the latter years of Art Nouveau. Later works made increasing use of veneers, lacquer and inlays, and fewer carved details – an early Follot signature – appeared. Follot designed carpets, textiles, ceramics, metalwork, jewellery and wallpaper, the latter of which his family's firm produced, and always had a keen interest in creating multiple components of an interior. He left Pomone in 1928, at about which time he became co-director, along with Serge Chermayeff, of the Paris branch of the London furniture emporium, Waring & Gillow; together they designed some sixty model rooms for that firm.

Follot's designs were closely identified with Pomone for the near-decade he directed the atelier, but other well-known designers also made their mark on the firm – and the buying public. Albert Guénot (b. 1894) began working for Pomone in 1923, first as a sculptor-designer, then as shop foreman. In 1932 he succeeded René Prou, Follot's successor, as director. He often collaborated on interiors with both men, those done with Follot generally more decorated than those with Prou, which were dominated by furniture wholly sheathed, without ornamentation, with the handsomest native woods (including figured cherrywood, elm and walnut). René Prou (1889-1947) was described as early as 1912 as the foremost decorator 'in the modern taste'. His sturdy, straight-forward carved- and veneered-wood forms were distinguished by discreet decoration (if any), and he also became enamoured of forged-metal furniture (c. 1930). Like many other Art Deco designers, he contributed interiors to several ocean liners of the French Line and others, and he also designed for trains – elegant, wood-panelled compartments for luxury *wagons-lits*, as well as *wagons-salons*. He received several significant foreign commissions, among them a dining room for the Waldorf-Astoria hotel in Manhattan, a council room in Geneva's Society of Nations and interiors for the Mitsubishi department store in Tokyo.

The last of the *grands magasins* to establish an atelier was Le Louvre, whose Studium was set up under the direction of Etienne Kohlmann (b. 1903) in 1923. Unlike the other three ateliers, Studium's interiors were almost uniformly in the Modernist rather than the high-style Art Deco vein, always in the best of taste for a discerning clientele, but with no vestigial c. 1910-15 ornamentation. The fact that Kohlmann and most of his Studium colleagues were nearly a generation younger than Follot and Dufrêne meant that no lingering earlier elements of a fussy decorative style made an appearance in their room settings. Not that the furnishings were not classically inspired – slim, tapering legs might support a delicate lady's dressing table, a marquetry landscape might adorn a rich wood-veneered buffet – but such elements were subtle and discreet, never overpowering or loud. Other designers associated with Studium included Edouard-Joseph Djo-Bourgeois, a confirmed Modernist who nonetheless made use of precious woods in his minimalist Studium interiors, Maurice Matet, Pierre Lahalle, Georges Lavard and André Fréchet (the latter three created a living room and boudoir for Studium's pavilion at the 1925 Paris Exposition).

Mention should also be made of yet another Paris retail establishment which set up an atelier, namely, Au Bûcheron. Le Sylve was directed by Michel Dufet (1888-1985), who had previously founded the furniture-making firm M.A.M. (Mobilier Artistique Moderne, 1913-24), as well as having run a highly successful design firm in Rio de Janeiro, Red Star, which existed from 1928 to 1939. Art critic Léandre Vaillat also helped to run this atelier, whose interiors were strongly stamped with Dufet's style: straightforward, rectilinear shapes combined with sumptuous new substances, such as a stepped bookcase of maple sheathed in zinc.

Besides the ateliers of the four *grands magasins* and the interior-decorating-cum-design firms run by Ruhlmann, Süe et Mare, Dufet, D.I.M. and others, numerous other design establishments were set up in Paris in the twenties. Some of them were attached to retail stores, others were cabinet-makers-turned-designers or interior designers who worked with a wide variety of manufacturers and designers on a freelance basis. Athélia, the atelier of the Trois-Quartiers store, opened in late 1928 under the direction of Robert Block (in the early 1930s, he was succeeded by Paul Delpuech). Like many other establishments of the time, Athélia provided complete interior schemes to the public, from floor and wall coverings to furniture and lighting, and it was known for its richly veneered furniture, as well as its mirror-covered surfaces.

The Modernist designers, notably Le Corbusier, Pierre Jeanneret and Charlotte Perriand, were to make a mark on interior design that far outlasted the impact of the adherents of high-style Art Deco. But there were many Parisian designers of the period whose works bridged both the opulent and functional, who were quite comfortable mixing, say, tubular-steel-framed, leather-covered chairs with richly lacquered and veneered cabinets. Some, like Perriand, Djo-Bourgeois and Mallet-Stevens, could be called purists, in that any sort of decoration was more or less banned from their repertoires, but others, like Chareau and Dufet, felt free to mix a degree of luxuriousness (in materials) with sobriety (of form).

Besides Le Corbusier, Jeanneret and Perriand (who often worked as a team), Edouard-Joseph Djo-Bourgeois, Robert Mallet-Stevens, Pierre Chareau and Michel Dufet, the list of significant Modernist designers in the 1920s and 1930s is an impressive one, on which the names Eileen Gray, Francis Jourdain, René Herbst, Jean-Michel Frank, Paul Dupré-Lafon appear, as

Stéphany, a firm primarily known for its fabric and wallpaper designs, unveiled this decorator's office in the late 1920s. Except for its overstuffed leather chair, the room is a smart geometric essay, from the zigzag and rectangular patterns on the walls to the interesting tripartite wall lights.

well as a host of the less familiar, including Gabriel Guévrékian, Pierre Petit, Adrienne Gorska, Lucie Holt Le Son and Lucie Renaudot.

Eileen Gray (1878-1976), the self-taught Irish-born architect-designer who spent most of her adult working life in France, was one of the most hard-working, dedicated, adventurous yet modest of interior designers. Her first decorated interiors were almost certainly those of her own Paris flat, a second-floor apartment on the rue Bonaparte which she rented in 1907, bought in 1910 and kept as her Paris residence for the next 66 years, until her death. She changed its colours and furnishings over the years, but essentially kept the hall, living room, dining room, two bedrooms and kitchen simply, comfort-ably, practically decorated (although she never removed the incongruously ornate plaster mouldings from the ceilings). The rooms were usually painted white, although for a while her bedroom was black (but for a blue line dividing walls and ceiling), as was the kitchen.

The interiors Gray designed for others were, in line with the client's requests and lifestyles, richer and on the whole more stylized and harmonious than her own. Although she designed individual pieces for couturier Jacques Doucet, she did not create any interiors for the noted collector-connoisseur. Her first such commission came from another denizen of the world of fashion, Mme Mathieu-Lévy, who owned the modiste salon, Suzanne Talbot, and desired a 'radically new look' for her rue de Lota apartment, a task that took Gray four years to complete. Gray relished the idea of putting together a total, harmo-nious milieu, and the resultant rooms were undeniably luxurious yet radically simple. The flat's simplicity was in its line and general lack of fussy ornament and extraneous furnishings, but it took expert workmanship and thousands of man-hours to achieve such an effect. Lacquer was the key ingredient of the entire scheme, from the entry hall, where small lacquered-brick panels in gold, silver and matt grey covered the walls, to the salon, whose walls compris-ed black-lacquered panels covered with a silvered landscape-like geometrical motif and in which sat the celebrated 'Pirogue' sofa, a canoe-bed of lacquer and several shades of tortoiseshell. There was a parchment-covered ceiling light in the hallway, an ostrich-egg ceiling-light shade in the salon and 'dis-creet and relaxing lighting' elements throughout, as Mme Mathieu-Lévy had requested. There was a carpet woven with geometric motifs, and that in the salon was deep, soft black. A long, handsome bookcase in the salon, of tan and brown lacquer with grey, black and silver accents, also boasted a practical aspect: adjustable shelving. The overall atmosphere was luxurious, myste-rious, inviting, and the apartment was received with much enthusiasm by the owner and given much praise by the press. Surprisingly, Mme Mathieu-Lévy did not live long with Gray's design, for by the early 1930s, architect Paul Ruaud had redesigned it, albeit keeping much of Gray's furniture. She also created some new pieces for the renovated apartment, including white brick screens and two of the now-famous 'Bibendum' chairs, covered in white leather.

In 1922, when Eileen Gray was about halfway through the Mathieu-Lévy commission, she opened up Jean Désert, a shop in the Faubourg Saint-Honoré from which she ran her ever-expanding business (she had previously operated out of her home), which included not only furniture, lacquerwork, screens and rugs, but also, as her card read, 'Décoration et Installation d'Appartements'. Tasteful arrangements of furniture and whole room settings filled the shop, whose walls were simply painted white. The list of subsequent clients read like a Who's Who of Paris – artists, architects, royalty, couturiers, politicians. She finally started showing her works regularly in the salons, and her so-called Monte Carlo Room, a bedroom-boudoir displayed at the Fourteenth Salon des Artistes Décorateurs in 1923, caused a sensation. Unlike any other room on view, Gray's was dominated by screens, lacquerwork and the colours black and white (with a touch of red in the lacquer panels behind the black-lacquered bed, and blue in a glass lamp). A fur was thrown on the bed and parchment lamps abounded, including one standard version of lacquered wood and painted parchment that was part-tribal Africa, part futuristic fantasy. Several critics decried the strict formality and bizarre, eccentric motifs of this Cubist-inspired room (one called it 'funereal', another 'the daughter of Caligari in all its horror'), but those who might have been her harshest critics, her fellow designers, heaped a great deal of praise on it. Chareau, Mallet-Stevens and Francis Jourdain, among others, admired the modernity and simplicity of the Monte Carlo Room.

Gray continued to exhibit rooms at various salons, and also at the premier exhibition of the newly founded Union des Artistes Modernes, of which she was also a member, but she became increasingly preoccupied with architecture, with the idea of designing not only a dwelling on the inside, but its exterior as well, and from 1929, when the house she designed in the south of France for architect and critic Jean Badovici was completed, architecture became her passion. The year 1929 was also that of the Wall Street Crash and, luxury furniture not being especially saleable, Gray decided to close down Jean Désert. Her subsequent interiors – for E.1027, as Badovici's house was called, as well as for Badovici's rue Chateaubriand flat, for her own Tempe à Pailla in the south of France – were bereft of lacquer, which she had all but abandoned, and agleam with chromed metal.

Eileen Gray was not the only woman designing furniture and interiors in the Modernist style in Paris, and it is interesting to note that there were considerably more women working in the Moderne vein than in that of high-style Art Deco, which was a predominantly male bastion, as indeed

French design had traditionally been. Evelyn Wyld, an Englishwoman, and the American Elizabeth Eyre de Lanux lived and worked in Paris for many years. Wyld, an old family friend of Gray, worked for a while with her, supervising the manufacture of the carpets Gray designed (and also designing some of her own). After leaving Gray's shop, Jean Désert, and not on the best of terms with her colleague, Wyld began collaborating with Eyre de Lanux (she dropped her Christian name), a painter-journalist, whose many social contacts came to good use when the pair set up a design studio. They designed interiors for well-off Americans in Paris, and their rooms were distinguished by their earthy tones, geometric motifs and rich, varied textures of materials, such as pony-skin, cowhide, slate, terracotta, natural oak and raw silk.

Lucie Holt Le Son (b. 1899) was a painter and sculptor born in Philadelphia who began to contribute to interiors in Paris around 1925. Her interiors were distinguished for the silhouettes that appeared on the screens and wall panels, such as a 1928 travel-agency office shown at the Salon des Artistes Décorateurs, with handsome Modernist images of ocean liners, aeroplanes and trains covering painted and lacquered panelled walls. That setting also included chromed-metal and blue-tinted furniture designed by Holt Le Son, its forms strictly rectilinear, nonetheless evincing a chic elegance. Subsequent interiors included lacquered-wood furniture, but in the main Holt Le Son – who also received interior-design commissions from clients in her native country – was best known for her metallic furniture, complemented by carpets, upholstery and painted wall panels covered with strong abstract motifs.

Among the first major interior designs of Lucie Renaudot (d. 1939) were two tea rooms, the Tipperary and the Ça Ira, in Paris. Their furnishings were simple but chic tables and chairs of lacquered wood, and critics remarked on her 'feminine sensibility' and refined sense of scale. Many of Renaudot's 1920s interiors comprised furniture that was mass-produced, and the furniture-making firm P.A. Dumas made most of them. But she was not averse to evoking the past in some of her interiors, especially those displayed at major exhibitions, and one living room c. 1925 contained elegant furniture on tapering legs that was reminiscent of late-eighteenth-century English forms. She preferred to use elegant woods, sometimes in interesting juxtapositions (mottled amboyna with dark acajou, for instance). She designed interiors in Paris and in the French provinces, and also contributed to the design of the *Normandie*.

Adrienne Gorska (1899-1969), of Polish origin but Russian-born, studied architecture in Paris, where she married fellow architect Pierre de Montaut (with whom she often collaborated). Perhaps her best-known interiors were created for her sister, the fashionable Art Deco painter, Tamara de Lempicka, who bought a large rue Méchain apartment-cum-studio in 1929. Robert

American-born Lucie Holt Le Son was a painter whose interior designs appeared in Paris from 1925. The walls of this travel-agency office, from the 1928 Salon des Artistes Décorateurs, were painted with the kinds of smart, positive images that distinguished her work. The strongly rectilinear furniture was largely of chromed metal, and some pieces were tinted blue.

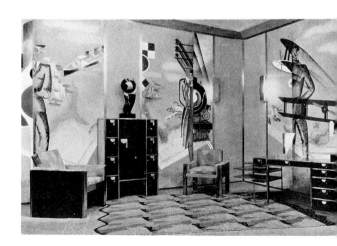

Charlotte Perriand, who frequently collaborated with Le Corbusier, designed this elegant Modernist dining room in 1928. The chairs, though of tubular metal, comfortably envelop and support their occupants with their two stuffed-leather components. Note how one end of the table is attached to the wall.

Mallet-Stevens provided most of its interior design, but Gorska created its entrance hall, a striking chrome and glass space, as well as its stunningly Moderne wood-panelled and chrome-accented bar.

Charlotte Perriand (b. 1903), like Eileen Gray, was an influential, innovative designer of furniture and interiors in the 1920s and 1930s, although their importance was not sufficiently recognized until decades later. Unlike Gray, however, the majority of Perriand's interior designs were cooperative efforts, with Le Corbusier and, sometimes, Pierre Jeanneret. She studied under Follot and Dufrêne at the Ecole de l'Union Centrale des Arts Décoratifs in the early 1920s and even exhibited furniture in the high-style Art Deco vein, but by 1927 she was designing aluminium and chromed-steel furniture, which largely made up her model room, 'Le Bar sous le toit' ('the bar under the roof'), shown at the 1927 Salon d'Automne. The bar first brought her to the attention of Le Corbusier, and soon after they were working together on *l'équipement pour l'habitation*, revolutionary furniture, including the famous 1929 'Chaise Longue', the 'Grand Confort', and assorted examples of no-nonsense, often built-in furniture. For about a decade, Perriand worked with Le Corbusier and his cousin, Jeanneret, designing furniture as well as 'equipping' interiors, including that of the Swiss pavilion of the Cité Universitaire.

The interiors created by Le Corbusier (born Charles-Edouard Jeanneret, 1887-1965), generally in collaboration with his cousin Pierre Jeanneret (1896-1967) and Charlotte Perriand, are not as well known nor indeed as significant as the individual objects and architectural projects he produced. Indeed, unlike other Modernist architect-designers, among them Mallet-Stevens, Herbst and Djo-Bourgeois, of whose *oeuvres* interior designing formed a major part, Le Corbusier was known primarily as an architect. Still, his joint efforts with Jeanneret and Perriand, notably the starkly functionalist interior of a villa at Ville d'Avray (1930) and his controversial Pavillon de l'Esprit Nouveau at the 1925 Paris Exposition, serve to illustrate well that significant trend in the interior design of the twenties and thirties that would, in the long run, far outlast those high-style Parisian room settings that had so entranced the city of *les années folles*. His 'industrial equipment', prefabricated cells and overall purist vision did not entirely eradicate interior design, but they led to the creation of a whole new vocabulary within the field.

Robert Mallet-Stevens (1886-1945), a trained architect and admirer of Mackintosh and Hoffmann (he was in fact the nephew of Adolphe Stoclet, who had commissioned the Viennese designers to create his Palais Stoclet in Brussels), began exhibiting interiors around 1912. Early settings showed a Viennese influence, and numerous subsequent designs, though not at odds with his previous creations, displayed a decidedly Modernist bent, especially in terms of the materials he used. He created several buildings and interiors for the 1925 Paris Exposition, and his Pavillon du Tourisme, with stained-glass by Louis Barillet, sculptures by his frequent collaborators (and clients), the Martel brothers, and furniture by Jourdain and Chareau, was largely Cubist-inspired, a bold gesture against high-style Art Deco. A later reaction against tradition was his founding in 1930, with other notable designers (including Herbst, Jourdain, Le Corbusier, Gray, Chareau and Djo-Bourgeois), of the Union des Artistes Modernes, of which he became the first president. Unlike Le Corbusier and other purists, Mallet-Stevens was not averse to using colour in his rooms, which was also not at odds with his attraction to the Dutch De Stijl movement. Any fussy design or ornament was eradicated from his later interiors, and geometry – in furniture shapes, floor-covering designs, lighting fixtures – became the rule. He was also fond of large empty spaces minimally furnished, a predilection, according to critic Léon Moussinac, inspired by Japanese interiors. A significant design project at Auteuil was creating an entire street of homes, including his own and that of the Martel brothers.

Another architect-designer whose Modernist works were related to those of Mallet-Stevens was Francis Jourdain (1876-1958), whose father, Frantz, was the architect of the Paris *grand magasin*, La Samaritaine (1905). A trained painter and printmaker, Jourdain turned to interior design around 1909. He won a prize at the 1911 Exposition in Turin (in the guise of *ensemblier*); a year later he set up Les Ateliers Modernes, which produced his furniture designs, and in 1919 he opened a retail shop for his furniture, Chez Francis Jourdain. Although his ideal was to produce affordable, mass-marketable furniture, his solid, rectilinear wooden pieces (and the occasional tubular-metal ones), most of them built-in, appealed primarily to an affluent clientele (this same dilemma had affected William Morris decades earlier, and many other idealistic designers since).

Although the later interiors of architect-decorator René Herbst (1891-1982) were Modernist in feel, some of his earliest designs, produced after he began to practice architecture in Paris in 1919, displayed characteristics of high-style Art Deco, such as an interior at the 1921 Salon d'Automne. The furniture forms in this den were basically geometric, but there were still vestigial curves apparent in them. Most of all, the silk-covered walls and upholstery were ablaze with a dense pattern of stylized blossoms. But this first stage of Herbst's design career was soon eclipsed by his dominant Modernist inclinations: from around 1925, he banished extraneous decoration from his schemes, soon incorporating tubular-metal chairs, pivoting drawers and other such Moderne elements into his repertoire.

Edouard-Joseph Djo-Bourgeois (1898-1937) studied under Mallet-Stevens, designed furniture and model rooms for both the Studium and Primavera ateliers, and often made use of textiles designed by his wife, Elise Djo-

Bourgeois, in his strongly Modernist interiors. Although his early 1920s room settings included veneered-wood pieces, later designs featured built-in furniture and tubular-nickel, varnished aluminium and other metallic surfaces. A villa he designed on the French Riviera was startlingly geometric, inside and out, the dining room devoid of ornament to the point of visual starvation. Nonetheless, such an extreme, dramatic room setting, dependent almost totally on form (comfort was not a great concern, and there was not a cushion in sight), took a great deal of daring to produce – and made one of the strongest Modernist statements ever.

Before he began to design his richly veneered furniture and later his interiors, Pierre Chareau (1883-1950) worked at Waring & Gillow, the London furniture makers, as a draughtsman. From 1919 he exhibited at the salons, and in 1924 he designed an office-study for Jacques Doucet (with African-derived furniture by Pierre Legrain). A handsome *bureau-bibliothèque* of his design featured in the Ambassade Française at the 1925 Paris Exposition, a room which also contained a sculpture by Jacques Lipchitz, a carpet by Jean Lurçat, textiles by Hélène Henry and stunning bookbindings by Legrain. The young Chareau had studied architecture, and many of his furniture pieces portray a sensitive relationship to their setting, such as beds and chairs that almost literally hug the floor. Chareau was especially fond of precious wood veneers, and ornament was all but banished from his repertoire. Subtle curves marked many of these early furniture pieces, but later examples tended to be rigorously geometric (these were often made of metal). Chareau was also greatly concerned with light, and created unusual, multiplaned shades that distributed artificial light in a pleasing manner. After 1925, Chareau was commissioned to create major room settings, both public and private, for a number of clients, including the entirety of the Grand Hôtel in Tours and the so-called Maison de Verre (House of Glass) for his friend, Doctor Jean Dalsace, in Paris (around 1919 he had designed a bedroom and study for Dalsace). In 1939 Chareau left Paris for New York, where he continued to design homes and interiors.

Another French Modernist, Jean-Michel Frank (1893-1941), also left Paris for New York prior to World War II, and spent his final years there. Frank, too, was a Modernist who was able to combine his love of beautiful materials – sharkskin, rare woods, vellum – with his preference for strict, geometric forms. In 1927, two rooms he designed for the Vicomte Charles de Noailles' Paris residence brought him acclaim: the walls of both were covered in tiles of glazed parchment, providing a suitably subtle setting for the plain, rectilinear but still elegant tables, sofa, chairs and cabinets.

Finally, three other designers of interiors in Paris deserve mention. All three were born at the turn of the century, which means they had no direct contact

A pure Modernist statement, this smoking room by René Herbst is wholly inhabited by tubular-metal furniture, from the chairs and tables to the bold, futuristic standard lamp. It dates from 1928.

with earlier Art Nouveau. Their room settings were pure Modernism, but, interestingly, all three evinced a love of beautiful, rich materials.

Gabriel Guévrékian (1900-1970) was a Turkish-born architect-decorator who worked for a time with Mallet-Stevens and later for D.I.M. He designed many private homes as well as shop interiors, including one of the latter for Sonia Delaunay at the 1925 Paris Exposition. His interiors often contrasted rich, dark-veneered wood against simple forms and stark white walls.

Paul Dupré-Lafon (1900-1971) served a wealthy clientele almost exclusively, among them members of the Dreyfus banking dynasty and those of the Hermès firm. His elegant furnishings featured straight lines and rich materials and were always impeccably produced. Unlike his colleagues, Dupré-Lafon shunned the salons, did not desire (or need) publicity and worked only on commission.

Pierre Petit (1900-1969), after studying at the Ecole Boulle, took a job with the Siégel firm, which specialized in installing shops. While there, he designed furniture, lighting fixtures, even metal grilles, so when he went out on his own, in 1928, he was well-equipped to design complete interior schemes. He turned increasingly to Cubist-inspired forms and metal furniture and distinguished himself, too, for daring colour contrasts: for instance, light-wood furniture combined with bright-red, fabric-covered walls.

The early twentieth-century couturier, Paul Poiret, also directed his vast design talents to creating interiors, via his Atelier Martine. His influences included German, Viennese and Oriental design, as well as the Ballets Russes. At the 1925 Paris fair his pavilion comprised three barges on the Seine; these two rooms were part of that floating display. The dining room (*below*) combined the rectilinear forms of Secession Vienna with bold Ballets Russes hues. But for the square chair, the verdant sitting room on the *Amours* houseboat (*right*) had a lush, joyful, jungle-like atmosphere. Big puff pillows provided casual seating; palm trees and other flora covered the walls, and a carpet awash with big, rippling fronds brightened the sunken floor area.

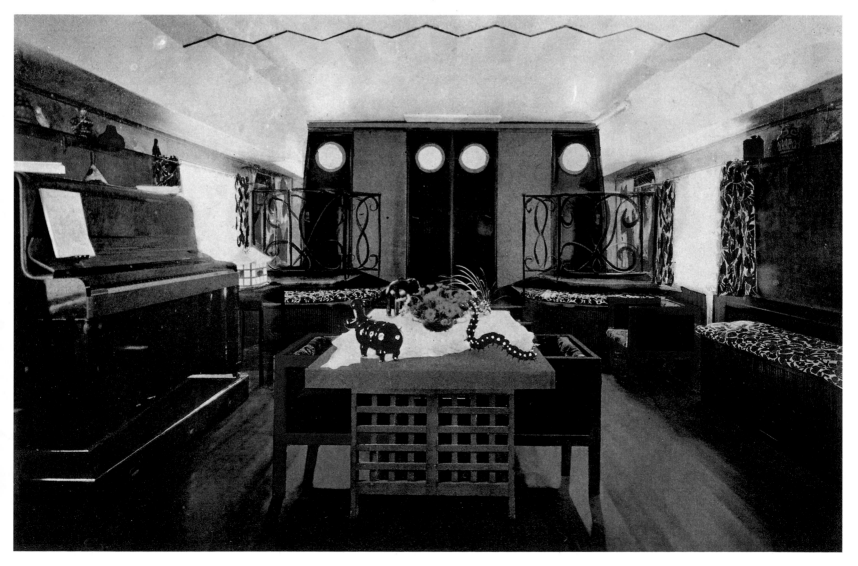

In the striking stairwell area of Doucet's studio (*above*), gleaming metal birds perch on the geometric-railed bannister by Hungarian-born sculptor Joseph Csaky and on the landing is a Constantin Brancusi head. Louis Marcoussis, a Polish-born painter who designed carpets for the Aubusson workshops, created the cream, red and black area rug at the foot of the illustration.

Couturier Jacques Doucet's studio at Neuilly was one of the premier showcases for Art Deco furnishings and modern art. In a corner of the 1929 studio (*opposite*) are a large painting by Marie Laurencin, a red-leather armchair by Pierre Legrain and a green- and silver-lacquered window blind with avian scene by Hecht. In front of the blind is an ebony table (*right*) by Rose Adler, elaborately inlaid with sharkskin arranged in a stylized cityscape design. On top of the table is a rock-crystal sculpture (*above right*) on a silver, silver-gilt and enamel base by Hungarian-born Gustave Miklos. Today both pieces are reunited in the collection of the Virginia Museum of Fine Arts, Richmond, whose Sydney and Frances Lewis Collection also includes other Doucet pieces.

The bold Cubist designs on some of the ceilings in Doucet's villa are clearly seen in this photograph (*opposite*). The sharkskin-covered cabinet on the left is by Pierre Legrain; over it hangs a painting by Matisse and a carpet by Gustave Miklos is on the floor.

This room (*below*) in Doucet's studio could have constituted a small museum with its outstanding paintings and sculpture – note Douanier Rousseau's *The Snake Charmer*, the Modigliani portrait and the Braques. Not only is the fine art skilfully arranged with the decorative pieces, but indeed they complement and enhance each other. For instance, Marcel Coard's rosewood, ivory and leather sofa (*left*), with its wood carved to resemble tropical rattan, is draped with a wild-animal skin and overhead is an appropriate primeval scene. Also in the room are Eileen Gray's African-inspired round table and a massive glass door by René Lalique.

In 1927 Ruhlmann designed this ballroom (*opposite*) for the Chambre de Commerce, with massive ribbed pilasters, two rows of six crystal-beaded chandeliers and, over the door at the back, Joseph Bernard's bas-relief, *La Danse*. The master deftly created a grand, harmonious space compatible with its Second Empire setting, the Hôtel Potocki. The chairs in this contemporary photograph are not by Ruhlmann but nonetheless blend nicely with their older setting.

Ruhlmann was as adept at creating practical but handsome offices and workspaces as he was opulent salons. The 1929 office of M. Haardt in the Citroën factory (*above*) contained sturdy oak furniture, the desk with matching lamp straightforward and functional, the chairs covered with red leather. The room was dominated by Choukaieff's bold mechanist painting. The reception room from a sanitation firm (*right*), with its curved, wood-panelled walls and rounded chair and table, presented a hushed but warm atmosphere of efficiency and comfort. The rolltop desk at the rear has bronze details, not the usual ivory touches.

Published in *Harmonies, Intérieurs de Ruhlmann*, this 1924 *pochoir* illustration depicts the bedroom of Baronne Henri de Rothschild in the Château de la Muette (*above*). The colour scheme, although not true-to-life (as was the case with most hand-tinted or *pochoir* plates), is basically correct, i.e., Ruhlmann's dark-veneered, ivory-inlaid and light-upholstered furniture set against light-coloured walls. Note the fan-shaped alabaster wall light, so common in the master's *oeuvre*, and the dressing table on the left, with the classical urn carved on the side.

Ruhlmann's bathrooms were every bit as elegant as his public rooms. This treatment for a marble-sheathed *salle de bain* (*opposite*), a *pochoir* print, was published in Editions Albert Lévy's *Répertoire du Goût Moderne* in the late 1920s.

D.I.M. (Décoration Intérieure Moderne) was a Paris design firm sometimes known by the names of its principals, Joubert et Petit. Philippe Petit's 1925 rendering of a Paris dining roof (*left*) is at once down-to-earth and elegant. It has a refined sense of geometry and the colour combination of blue and gold, along with the dark wood of the furniture, is harmonious and rather unusual. The 1924 bedroom (*below left*), also drawn by Petit, is an altogether loftier space, with its beige, russet and brown tones, exaggerated parabolic headboard and decorative upper wall panels under a high ceiling. The nicely furnished circular sitting area leading to the sleeping alcove in the *c.* 1930 D.I.M. bedroom (*below*) is cool-toned yet welcoming, providing a cosy, intimate space in a largely dramatic setting.

Armand-Albert Rateau was given free rein to make use of his highly personal design repertoire by his premier client, fashion designer Jeanne Lanvin. He designed the bedroom (*right*) for Mme Lanvin in 1920-22; today it is reconstructed in the Musée des Arts Décoratifs in Paris. Its walls are covered in cornflower-blue silk, with marguerite blossoms embroidered in white and gold threads; it features two avian-embellished standard lamps and a low table in green-patinated bronze – exotic forms inspired by both classical antiquity and the Orient.

Rateau's lavish, exotic bathroom for Jeanne Lanvin (*below*) was an essay in flora and fauna, from bird-shaped taps to the carved stucco wall panel, with its forest scene, behind the bath. The bathtub and basin are of cream Siena marble; the floor is of a crisp, geometric design, while the metalwork – mirror, lamp, fixtures – is of Rateau's favourite material, patinated bronze. He designed a similar bathroom earlier for the Duchess of Alba in Madrid.

Eric Bagge, although mainly an architect and designer of objects (jewellery, fabric, wallpaper), also created furniture and interiors, like this office (*left*) from the mid 1920s. Bagge's style began in the opulent Art Deco vein – ivory details, flower baskets and veneered pieces – but later interiors, such as this office, were markedly geometric.

André Groult's living room (*opposite above*) presents an earthy-toned mélange of pieces, including a chequerboard-veneered piano, sturdy console table, geometric-patterned screen and carpet, and nicely rounded mirror and scroll-side chairs. The grey, green and black palette of the 1924 dining room (*below*) complements the painting of a fashionable angling couple. But for the stylized floral motifs on the sideboard, this classically elegant room could almost date from a century earlier.

These three interiors are by André Groult, a thoughtful decorator often subtly inspired by classical French design. Although equally adept at creating living, dining and men's rooms, he is probably best known for his pale-toned, overtly feminine spaces, like the young girl's room in blue (*right*) and the powdery pink bedroom (*above*) which was displayed in the Ambassade Française at the 1925 fair. With its Marie Laurencin painting and sharkskin-covered and ivory-inlaid bed, chairs and anthropomorphic cabinet, the Chambre de Madame was an exercise in pale tones that emitted a warm aura.

The first Paris department store to set up an atelier was Le Printemps, whose Primavera studio was established in 1913 by René Guilleré (his wife, Charlotte Chauchet-Guilleré, was its long-time manager). Louis Sognot, one of Primavera's resident designers, created the two drawing rooms seen here. Although his later interiors made liberal use of chromed metal and rigid geometric forms, most were filled with fine veneered furniture. Note the sympathetic mix of both curvilinear and rectilinear forms in both rooms, as well as the boldly patterned abstract rugs.

Murals painted by S. Olesiewicz with cheerful, quasi-Cubist classical figures flank the dining room (*above*) designed by Marcel Guillemard and displayed in Le Printemps' Primavera pavilion at the 1925 Paris fair. The furniture is of golden lemonwood, and the room's colour scheme is in shades of cream, yellow and grey.

The red- and black-dominated young man's bedroom (*left*) by Marcel Guillemard, was furnished by Primavera. Note especially the centre table with wrought-iron base, the squares of abstract designs on the carpet, the built-in bed, the striped wall covering and the sturdy rectilinearity of the decidedly masculine room.

Maurice Dufrêne was director of La Maîtrise, Galeries Lafayette's design studio, for over twenty years and was exposed to the undulating lines of Art Nouveau early in his career, though his later creations tended to the rectilinear. His aim above all was to maintain the highest traditions of French design, concurrently making use of novel materials. This 1919 rendering of a Maurice Dufrêne bedroom (*left*) appeared in the publication *Feuillets d'Art*.

The curve is the predominant motif in Dufrêne's lady's bedroom (*below left*) in the Maîtrise pavilion at the 1925 Paris fair. The veneered furniture is of white maple and lemonwood, and a rippling but rigidly regular curvilinearity marks their shapes, as well as the border on the mirror and the ceiling painting.

Dufrêne's dining room (*below and opposite below*) seen in both a period black-and-white photograph and a coloured print, was displayed in La Maîtrise's pavilion at the 1925 Paris fair; Gabriel Englinger collaborated with him on its design.

Grey walnut and palissander furniture fills this serene, earth-toned study-office (*above left*); it was designed by Paul Follot, director of the Pomone atelier, in whose 1925 fair pavilion the room was shown. Delicate floral motifs covered the carpet and curtains, and gilded relief sculptures in the frieze, by Do Canto, depicted a sylvan scene with cherubs amid rich flora and fauna.

André Fréchet, along with Lahalle et Levard, created this lush, pink-tinted reception hall (*above right*) for the Studium-Louvre pavilion at the 1925 Paris Exposition. The lemonwood furniture was covered in silk damask, and relief decoration, such as the fronds on the table legs, was by Laurent Malclès.

The department store Au Bûcheron started up its atelier, Le Sylve, under the direction of Michel Dufet, who specialized in sumptuous furniture and new substances. The 1931 advertisement (*left*) features a polished-zinc desk and steel chairs covered in zebra skin; the office was a commission from a mining firm, the Compagnie Asturienne des Mines. Sculptor-turned-*ensemblier* Jules Leleu's simple but striking 1931 advertisement (*below*) appeared in a French publication, but he also advertised in the English journal *The Studio*. A traditionalist inspired by eighteenth-century French design, Leleu used the finest, most luxurious materials to embellish his furniture, which in the main was cheaper to buy than that of Ruhlmann and Süe et Mare.

Galeries Lafayette, the Paris *grand magasin*, opened its atelier La Maîtrise in 1921. At the 1925 Paris fair, studio director Maurice Dufrêne and other designers created rooms for the atelier's pavilion, three of which are seen here (*opposite above*). On the left is Gabriel Englinger's and Suzanne Guiguichon's opulent, shocking-pink boudoir; in the middle is Dufrêne's dining room and on the right is a wide interior view showing Dufrêne's hall.

The numerous design and decoration journals published in Europe in the 1920s and 1930s provided advertising space for *ensembliers* and design firms. This line drawing (*opposite below*) is for the interior-design firm Dominique, formed in 1922 by André Domin and Marcel Genevrière.

Eileen Gray's Monte Carlo room (*above*) caused a sensation at the fourteenth Salon des Artistes Décorateurs in 1923. Dominated by lacquerwork, screens, and black and white (with a touch of red in the panels behind the bed, and blue in a glass lamp), it was unlike any room on view. One of its highlights was a lacquered-wood and painted-parchment standing lamp (*right*), which was part tribal Africa, part futurist fantasy. One critic called the room 'funereal', another 'the daughter of Caligari in all its horror', but Gray's esteemed colleagues – Chareau and Mallet-Stevens among them – admired its modernity and simplicity.

A room in Mme Mathieu-Lévy's apartment (*opposite*): although Eileen Gray's original dark screens and wall panels were replaced in Paul Ruaud's 1930s renovation – an allover whitewashing of the flat – much of Gray's furniture remained. The focal point of this minimally decorated space is the canoe-shaped 'Pirogue' sofa, inspired in part by the Ballets Russes' *Schéhérazade* and covered with matt-gold cushions. Gray created three versions of this 'boat bed'; another, its interior sheathed with silver leaf, can be seen *opposite above*.

This 1933 photograph shows the Paris flat of Eileen Gray's client, Mme Mathieu-Lévy, after Gray's 1920s interiors were superseded by those of Paul Ruaud. Gone was Gray's dusky, mysterious milieu, but she still agreed to contribute objects to the flat's chic, fur-strewn reincarnation. Two 'Bibendum' chairs appear in the room, and in the centre is her tobacco-coloured sofa. The opulent red- and yellow-lacquered 'Serpent' chair wears a leopard skin, and a white brick screen is in the doorway on the left.

Early Mallet-Stevens interiors, even a sitting room shown at the 1921 Salon d'Automne (*right*), were far more decorative than his better-known later creations, such as the 1929 dining room. The early room features an abundance of floral motifs – on the upper walls and ceiling, on the pillows, carved on the matching mirrors and tables – plus a scattering of pillows, overstuffed seating and an overall air of cosy, cheerful comfort. The chromed-metal and veneered-wood forms and fixtures in the later room (*below*) can be said to embody the 'implacable rigidity' of which some of his critics accused him (although he was fond of bright colours and no doubt they helped brighten up this rectilinear space).

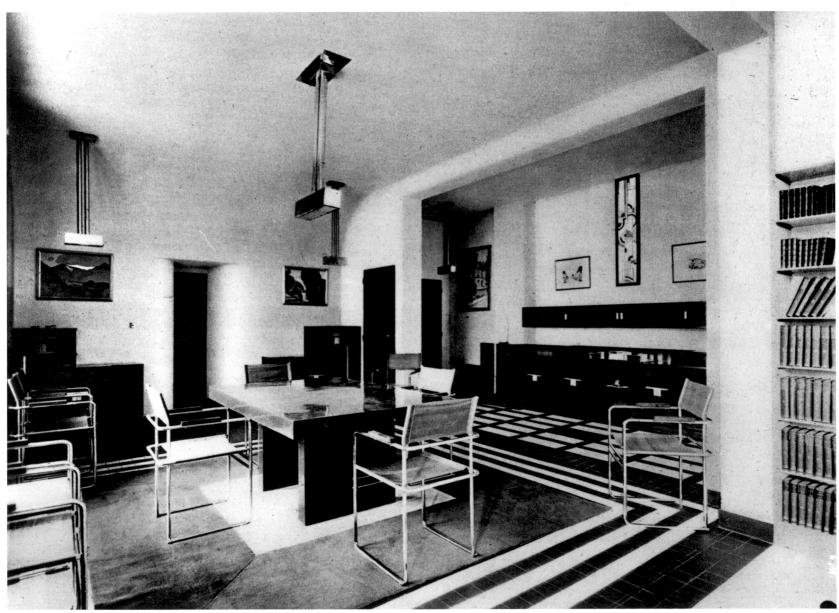

Robert Mallet-Stevens was an admirer of both the Vienna and Glasgow schools, and his early rooms often showed their influence. Subsequent interiors, though not at odds with his previous creations, displayed a strong Modernist bent. A significant *c.* 1930 project was to create an entire street of Auteuil homes, including his own. The sitting room (*opposite*) with its areas of yellow in a dark wood- and metal-dominated space, is from the Mallet-Stevens' residence.

The dining room of the Mallet-Stevens' residence had seating fabric by Hélène Henry and a carved-lacquer screen by Jean Dunand.

The strong Modernist tendencies of Edouard-Joseph Djo-Bourgeois, whose interior designs grew more severe and minimal with time, can be seen in these three photographs. The office-library (*top*), exhibited in the Studium-Louvre pavilion at the 1925 Paris fair, is colourful and comfortable, its solid hues offset by patterned rugs, drapes and upholstery (by P. Demaria). At the 1926 Salon d'Automne, however, Djo-Bourgeois showed a dining room (*centre*) with a more rigid, planar bent; even the square and triangle motifs on the curtains and carpet were somewhat subdued. Most severe of all is the c. 1929 dining room (*bottom*) designed for a French Riviera villa. Devoid of ornament to the point of visual starvation, this extreme and dramatic ghost of a room is dependent almost totally on form, with not a cushion in sight.

This elegant bathroom-cum-dressing room (*left*) with proportions as lofty as those in a Ruhlmann interior, was created by Michel Roux-Spitz *c.* 1929. Its fittings are of sycamore, its floor is covered with glass-paste mosaics and the bold geometric designs on the floor and corner screen – not to mention the fur rug – give the room an air of luxurious modernity.

The capacious *c.* 1930 bathroom (*right*) was designed for a Paris house by Paul Colin, who was perhaps best known for his posters of Josephine Baker's Revue Nègre. The walls are painted grey, but for green tiles in the alcove enclosing the green tub, and the floor is covered with red and black mosaic. The furniture is chromium-plated tubular metal, and illumination is provided by a square ceiling light, tube lighting over the two full-length mirrors, panels inset on either side of the tub – and a floor-to-ceiling window.

In the mid 1920s Francis Jourdain designed the two children's rooms seen here. The furniture in the nursery (*opposite below*) is light-toned and the room has an overall air of levity and charm, as in the wall mural, with swirls of peach smoke floating upwards from the houses appearing out of the moulding. The small circular carpet and sprinkling of pillows are pure Art Deco touches, although Jourdain was more the spare, functional Modernist than opulent, high-style *ensemblier*. The second room (*opposite above*) is altogether bolder and more rectilinear. With its array of fretwork and chequerboard motifs, it could almost be from Secessionist Vienna.

Architect-designer Francis Jourdain began creating interiors around 1909, in 1919 opening a retail shop for his furniture. His ideal was to produce affordable, mass-market pieces, but his largely wooden, built-in furniture appealed mainly to an affluent clientele. His *c.* 1929 drawing room (*below*) is defiantly Modernist, even down to the De Stijl-like glass panels set in the wall, but still chic and inviting. Hélène Henry contributed textiles to the room (wall and pillow coverings, upholstery); the table is lacquered and the geometric carpet is by Myrbor.

Modernist designer Jean-Michel Frank was able to combine his love of beautiful materials with his preference for strict, geometric forms. His 1927 interiors for the Paris residence of the Vicomte Charles de Noailles, three views of which are seen here, brought him wide acclaim. The walls were covered in large tiles of glazed parchment, providing a suitably subtle setting for the plain, rectilinear but still elegant sofa, chairs and cabinets. Note especially the cabinet in the sitting room (*below*) and another elsewhere (*left*), both sheathed with straw veneer arranged in a pattern of multiple diamonds.

From 1919 Pierre Chareau showed at the Paris salons, and in 1924 he designed an office-study for Jacques Doucet (*above*). The crisp, rectilinear room featured furniture by Pierre Legrain, some – like the chair and stool on the left – African-inspired. A much more Modernist stool can be seen in Chareau's *c.* 1925 bathroom (*left*), a warm, angled, airy space in earthy shades of gold and russet offset by deep blue.

The all-glass London bathroom of dancer Tilly Losch, designed in 1932 by Paul Nash (1979 reconstruction by Julian Feary and original contractors James Clark, Eaton & Son).

CHAPTER 4

STREAMLINE MODERNE
THE ART DECO INTERIOR WORLDWIDE

The true domestic Art Deco interior arguably existed only in France, from *c.* 1915 to 1930, in the private homes, in the regular salon exhibitions and, most notably, in the 1925 Paris Exposition, the premier showcase of *le style moderne.* However, the interiors designed and promoted by Ruhlmann, Follot, Groult, Süe et Mare and the Modernists Chareau, Frank, Gray and Mallet-Stevens exerted a great influence on many interiors that appeared in the United States, Great Britain, elsewhere on the Continent, including Eastern Europe, and even in such far-flung locales as South America, Australia and India, from *c.*1925 to the late 1930s. Elements of both the high-style Parisian Art Deco and its Modernist antidote, promulgated by Le Corbusier and the Union des Artistes Modernes, permeated interior design and decoration in many other countries.

DOMESTIC INTERIORS in the United States displayed a much wider range of styles and influences than those elsewhere. Besides French-inspired room settings – some in fact executed by Parisian designers themselves – there were those largely indebted to Viennese design, and likewise German- and Scandinavian-based interiors. Even the fantasy-laden style of Hollywood sets filtered down to actual interiors, and of course elements of exuberant skyscraper architecture were adapted to more intimate, but no less dramatic, room settings. And iconoclastic figures like Frank Lloyd Wright continued to work in distinctive but ever-evolving styles, which also affected the styles of their contemporaries.

New York was the natural habitat for many of America's premier designers working in the various modern idioms of the 1920s and 1930s styles. However, just as in London – and for that matter, Paris as well – tried-and-true traditional styles died hard with the moneyed class, and where there was Syrie Maugham in London, there was Elsie de Wolfe (1885-1950) in Manhattan. An actress who became a decorator in her late thirties, de Wolfe was also a pre-eminent society hostess in New York, hence there was no shortage of clients once she set up her business around 1904. Her decorative, feminine style combined eighteenth-century furniture forms with flowery (and 'cheap and cheerful') chintzes and at times even daring colour combinations (including a medley of pastels and a dichromatic black-and-white scheme).

Paul T. Frankl (1887-1958), who had trained as an architect in Europe, was one of the most original of the designers working in New York during the same period. A native of Vienna, he came to the United States in 1914, first working on stage sets. He opened his own gallery in East 48th Street in 1922, and by the end of the decade he was a huge success, creating some of New York's most distinctive, exuberant and luxuriant furniture and interior designs. His best-known pieces were the so-called skyscraper bookcases and cabinets, their stepped silhouettes echoing those of Manhattan's ever-rising edifices, and those in the Orientalizing style, some lacquered, gilt and silvered in the Japanese manner, others – tables and chairs with pierced openwork, for instance – actually assuming Chinese-inspired forms (he had in fact visited the Far East).

Donald Deskey (b. 1894), who had produced some hand-painted screens for the Frankl Gallery in 1927, had a few years later become one of his former employer's biggest rivals in popularity and number of commissions. Deskey studied architecture in California and painting in Chicago, New York and then Paris, taking on an assortment of jobs in between his schooling. He returned from France in 1926 and the next year set up Deskey-Vollmer, Inc., with Phillip Vollmer. The interior-design firm created window displays for retail establishments, model rooms for various exhibitions and actual interior schemes for notable New Yorkers, including Adam Gimbel (head of Saks Fifth Avenue), Abby Aldrich Rockefeller, Helena Rubinstein (for whom Frankl, incidentally, had designed a salon, his first major commission after opening his gallery) and drama critic Gilbert Seldes (who wrote a *New Yorker* profile of Deskey in 1933). Deskey's most renowned commission came in 1932, for the interiors of Radio City Music Hall.

Unlike Frankl, Deskey was much more Modernist in his leanings, both in terms of style and materials. He had been to the 1925 Paris Exposition and had been impressed by much of what was on view, but it was the distinctively modern forms, materials and methods of Le Corbusier, the Bauhaus and even De Stijl that influenced most of his furniture and objects, epecially those mass-produced pieces on which he concentrated more and more in the 1930s. Obviously, Deskey's luxurious private-residence commissions included many one-off, custom-made objects. Gimbel's study, for instance, conceived in shades of brown, tan and yellow, comprised custom-made furnishings of stainless steel and other metals, with corkboard walls, copper ceiling and linoleum floor. Indeed, as with the interiors of many of the French designers he had seen two years earlier at the 1925 Paris Exposition, Deskey was playing the role of the *ensemblier* in the case of the Gimbel flat and other private commissions to follow.

Other top industrial designers in the United States were designing interiors as part of their broad repertoire of creations. Walter von Nessen, Gilbert Rohde, Walter Dorwin Teague and Russel Wright all worked out of New York City, and all achieved renown and success in their multiple endeavours. Von Nessen (1889-1943) was concerned primarily with the design of metal furniture and objects, such as ashtrays and lamps, but he also created the occasional interior in his strict but elegant Modernist mode. Von Nessen, who was born in Berlin, had studied design with Bruno Paul and designed furniture in

Donald Deskey's firm, Deskey-Vollmer, produced this selection of objects *c.* 1928. Screen, wastebasket, table lamp, even cigarette and match holder are either shaped like or decorated with bold machine-part-like motifs, though obviously 'glamourized' for the discerning client.

Stockholm from 1919 to 1923, before setting up Nessen Studio in New York City.

Gilbert Rohde (1894-1944), a native New Yorker, received no formal education but worked at a variety of art- and design-related jobs (cartoonist, illustrator, photographer) before travelling to Europe in 1927, where he observed and admired French and German applied arts. Upon his return to New York, he started making tables of chromium-plated metal and Bakelite in an atelier he had set up in 1929. In the 1930s he designed tubular-metal, wooden and even wicker furniture that was made by, among others, the Herman Miller Furniture Company, the Troy Sunshade Company and the Heywood-Wakefield Company, as well as complete interiors, for exhibitions (including the 1934 Exhibition of Contemporary American Industrial Art at The Metropolitan Museum) and for actual clients (the Modernist-chic penthouse flat of Norman Lee in Greenwich Village's Sheridan Square).

Rohde applied himself to creating useful, attractive, economical interior designs, the elements of which could be mass-produced by the big furniture companies. To this end, he was a major force to be reckoned with in Grand Rapids (the Michigan location of many furniture manufacturers), and his often multifunctional designs ended up in many an American home, even in the Depression-wracked 1930s.

An industrial designer whose career began in the art department of a New York advertising agency, Walter Dorwin Teague (1883-1960) went on to design cameras for Eastman Kodak, glassware for Steuben, as well as the Marmon 16 automobile, cash registers, Texaco petrol stations, an X-ray unit, an aluminium and Lucite armchair, Pullman cars and numerous pavilions and displays for the 1939-40 New York World's Fair. In 1933, he designed his Madison Avenue studio, resulting in 'a marriage of functionalism and sharp color contrasts', according to one critic. The black-and-white theme of the studio was later extended by Teague to the foyer of the Executive Lounge of the Ford Building at the 1933 Century of Progress Exhibition in Chicago.

Russel Wright (1904-1976), who studied both painting and architecture, began his career designing stage sets. In 1927 he set up his own design business, eventually producing a wide variety of objects, from fabrics and flatware, to china and wallpaper. He designed a practical line of furniture for Heywood-Wakefield, called 'Flexible Modern' because of its versatility and modular nature (a three-piece sofa, for instance, could be arranged any number of ways). Like Teague, he visited Europe in the 1920s, taking in the various manifestations of modern design in France and Germany, absorbing most of all the straightforward, no-nonsense designs of Le Corbusier and Mallet-Stevens. Wright made extensive use of metals in both his individual objects – his chromium-plated pewter cocktail shaker, with its strong Machine Age

This bathroom featured in a 1936 American advertisement for Armstrong's linoleum floors. Ivory linoleum covered the walls, a plaid pattern was on the floor and even the tub was faced with black 'Linowall', the same material making up the panel behind it, which was inlaid with stylized floral motifs. Smart modern touches included the tubular-metal stool, cylindrical light beside the sink and spherical ceiling light.

silhouette, could be considered a symbol of its time – and his interior schemes.

Though not known for their interiors, Raymond Loewy (1893-1986) and John Vassos (b. 1898) were two versatile industrial designers who created room settings worth a mention. Vassos designed a handsome studio for photographer Margaret Bourke-White around 1933, its built-in components, according to a contemporary journal, 'as conveniently and economically planned as those in a ship's cabin'. Not strictly formal and rectilinear, the office's plate-glass desk top, chair back and other surfaces were smoothly curved. For his own Manhattan penthouse, Loewy – originator of the green-glass Coca Cola bottle and countless twentieth-century advertising icons – designed dramatic but practical interiors: the entrance lobby featured a black linoleum floor, yellow walls and grey-painted furniture with chromium trim, and a corner of the living room (which had two walls painted oyster white, the other two light gold) centred on an unusual white-painted fireplace, the left side right-angled and enclosing a single recessed bookshelf, the right side gently curving around the hearth.

Two noted designers of interiors, among other things, in 1920s and 1930s Manhattan were Joseph Urban (1872-1933) and Winold Reiss (1886-1953), both of whom were *émigrés* from Europe. Urban, a native of Vienna, began his career in Europe as an architect (he created a palace for the Khedive of Egypt in 1895). He first journeyed to the New World in 1904, when he designed the Austrian pavilion for the Louisiana Purchase Exposition in St. Louis. He came back again, this time for good, in 1911, settling in New York and pursuing a versatile design career.

Winold Reiss, born in Karlsruhe and educated in Munich, emigrated to America in 1913. He taught painting, founding a school in Woodstock, New York, in 1919, and also helped set up the magazine, *The Modern Art Collector*. His first interior-design commission, for the Crillon restaurant in Manhattan, also came in 1919, and many other jobs, mostly for hotels, restaurants and other public spaces, followed. Reiss's interiors were highly reminiscent of Viennese design, relying as they so often did on grid patterns, light colours and rectilinear forms.

Wolfgang and Pola Hoffmann were another European couple designing objects and interiors in 1920s New York. Hoffmann (b. 1900) was the son of Josef, and his Polish-born wife (b. 1902), studied under Josef in Vienna. They opened a studio in New York in 1927, designing and making furniture, textiles, metalwork, and creating interiors as well, many incorporating versatile combination pieces for small urban dwellings. Few vestiges of Viennese design were evident in their work, which was characterized above all by practicality and functionalism. Ilonka Karasz (1896-1981) was yet another *émigré* (she came from Budapest with her sister, Mariska) to New York. The two often collaborated on textiles (Ilonka designing, Mariska executing them), but Ilonka also designed some handsome Modernist interiors.

Decorator Harriet E. Brewer (who often employed elegant furniture and accessories by Russian-born Alexander Kachinsky), Hugo Gnam, Jr., Robert Heller, architects George Howe & William Lescaze, Raymond E. Hood, Herbert Lippmann and Ely Jacques Kahn were just some of the others who provided discerning New Yorkers with chic, Modernist interiors. One other individual should be singled out, however, Eugene Schoen (1880-1957), a native New Yorker who studied architecture at Columbia University, met Otto Wagner and Josef Hoffmann while on a travel scholarship in Europe, set up his own architectural firm in 1905 and then branched out into interior decorating soon after seeing the 1925 Paris Exposition.

Although New York was the undisputed centre of *le style moderne* in the United States, significant contemporary domestic interiors were also designed elsewhere, notably in Illinois, Michigan and California. Chicago, for decades a centre of innovative architecture and design, was also the home base of Frank Lloyd Wright, to whom it was of the utmost importance to create buildings and interiors that echoed and were sympathetic to life in the twentieth century. Wright's own integrated interiors, most of which ascribed to the open plan, were some of America's premier examples of work by an *ensemblier*, though their forms, materials and overall looks reflected an earlier Arts and Crafts aesthetic more than a later Art Deco one.

But there were other Chicago-based designers working in the Modernist vein, including Abel Faidy, Hal Pereira, John Wellborn Root and Robert Switzer. Swiss-born Faidy (1894-1965), who emigrated to America in 1914, designed for retail stores before going the freelance route around 1926. His best-known interior, and one of the jazziest Moderne spaces in America, was the 1927 ensemble for the Chicago penthouse flat of Charles and Ruth Singletary.

Though a Chicago native, Philip Maher (1894-1981), whose father, George Washington Maher, was a noted architect, travelled often to Europe, ever absorbing Parisian, Scandinavian, English and other Continental design. John Wellborn Root, a senior partner in the architectural firm of Holabird & Root, was also committed to Modernist interiors, but more along Jazz Age than high-style Parisian lines. His own Chicago flat was agleam with chromed and glass furniture, though a model room he created for The Architect and the Industrial Arts exhibition at The Metropolitan Museum in 1929 was a satiny-soft, highly feminine woman's bedroom in shades of blue, grey and pewter. Robert Switzer and his partner, Harold O. Warner, set up Secession Ltd. in 1927, Chicago's first retail establishment offering solely modern decorative arts. Switzer had been a Holabird & Root employee before going into business

German-born Kem Weber lived in Southern California but was influenced by New York's skyline – note the architectonic shapes of the bookcase, screen and fireplace in this *c.* 1926-27 drawing, done for Barker Brothers. In fact, Weber's furniture was popular on both coasts.

with Warner, and it was a trip to Austria, Germany and Scandinavia that had whetted their appetites to go out on their own (the trip had stocked their showroom as well). In 1929 Secession designed an urban Moderne interior for Walter S. Carr and his family, and the inspiration for much of its custom-built furnishings was undeniably Viennese. Hal Pereira, who was also responsible for the glitzy interiors of cinemas, created a sparkling contemporary entrance hall and dining room for newlyweds James and Marjorie Hopkins in 1929-30. Mrs. Hopkins assisted him, and the results of their collaboration were an elegant exercise that was part Oriental, part high-style Paris.

Another Midwest-based architect displayed model rooms in the 1929 Metropolitan Museum show, The Architect and the Industrial Arts. He was Eliel Saarinen (1873-1950), the talented Finn who had emigrated to the United States in 1923, as a result of praise that was garnered from his entry in a *Chicago Tribune*-sponsored competition a year earlier (he came in second). From 1923 to 1924 he taught architecture at the University of Michigan, and a year later his longtime association with the Cranbrook Academy of Art in Bloomfield Hills, Michigan, began. Saarinen's early designs were firmly rooted in the light and/or painted woods and simple but elegant forms of Germany and Scandinavia and his subsequent American furniture and interiors developed this basic aesthetic further, often assuming as well quite decorative characteristics, some gleaned from Vienna and Paris.

In addition to a number of Frank Lloyd Wright houses (Aline Barnsdall's Hollyhock House of 1920 foremost among them), Los Angeles and environs boasted some outstanding interiors, the best-known by two markedly antithetical designers, the determinedly contemporary Karl Emanuel Martin ('Kem') Weber and the contentedly retrogressive T. H. Robsjohn-Gibbings, both of whom were European-born (other notable designers in California included Donald B. Kirby, Paul Laszlo, and architects Richard Neutra and R. M. Schindler).

Kem Weber (1889-1963), a native of Berlin, studied there with Bruno Paul, the furniture designer, from 1908 to 1910. He travelled to San Francisco in 1914 to help design the German pavilion of the Panama-Pacific Exposition, and was not allowed to return home when World War I broke out. He attempted to eke out a living as an interior designer, but anti-German sentiments ran high and he was compelled to take on other jobs – including poultry farming and lumberjacking – to survive. After the war, he moved south to Santa Barbara, where he set up a studio, and three years later he settled in Los Angeles, where he worked as a draughtsman for the design studio of Barker Brothers. He visited the Paris Exposition on a 1925-26 European sojourn, and what he saw there convinced him to start his own business, which he did in Hollywood in 1927, calling himself an industrial designer.

The tubular-steel furniture (*below*) drawn in 1934 by Los Angeles-based Kem Weber shows a kinship with much of the tubular-metal furniture being produced in Germany and elsewhere in Europe (Weber was in fact German-born). The designs were for the Lloyd Manufacturing Company in Michigan.

The so-called 'neo-classical art moderne' of T.H. Robsjohn-Gibbings, a Briton living in America, was in fact fiercely anti-Modernist. This *c.* 1937 lady's bedroom, from Casa Encantada in Bel Air, California, features a light-wood Hollywood bed with high-arched, reeded top connected to a pair of oval bedside tables, their tops surmounted by curving lamp arms carved with foliage. Also in the room were a burlwood cabinet, its doors carved with stylized palm branches and standing on gilt-metal lion-paw feet, and a camel-back settee with C-scroll supports carved with stylized wings, also on lion-paw feet.

Weber's goal was 'to make the practical more beautiful and the beautiful more practical', and the highly distinctive, flamboyant, yet eminently utilitarian pieces he designed more than fit the bill. Some of his sketches of interiors were positively dizzying in their array of zigzagged, markedly vertical screens, fireplaces, bookcases and other such furniture. But photographs of actual interiors, such as a twin-bedded room of *c.*1929 in Beverly Hills, depict well-designed, harmonious, comfortable and sparkling Modernist spaces. Although based on the opposite coast, Weber was a frequent exhibitor in New York; for instance, he was one of several Americans asked to take part in R. H. Macy's International Exposition of Art in Industry in May 1928 (he showed a space-saving '6 rooms in 3' display, custom-made for urban survival). He was deeply interested in helping to solve the many problems facing city dwellers, as well as improving mass-production techniques in the manufacture of furniture. And, although arresting, even somewhat playful designs were part of his repertoire, the outward aspects of *art moderne* were, in his opinion, quite insignificant compared to its functional, practical sides.

At the opposite end of the spectrum from Weber's designs were the 'neo-classical art moderne' creations (as recent auction catalogues have referred to them) of Terence Harold Robsjohn-Gibbings (1905-1976), an Englishman who started out as an antiques dealer in his native country. He then moved to New York around 1930, where he found considerable success as an interior decorator and designer. About seven years later, he created the interiors of Casa Encantada in Bel Air, California, for Mrs. J.O. Weber (in 1952 the home, complete with furnishings, was bought by hotelier Conrad Hilton), without doubt the high point of his design career. T.H. Robsjohn-Gibbings is so closely identified with this West Coast dwelling that he is thought of as a quintessential Californian decorator, but in fact he designed furniture for the mass-market (produced by the Widdicomb Furniture Company of Grand Rapids, Michigan) in the 1940s, as well as interior schemes for clients on both coasts and in Europe as well.

ALTHOUGH GREAT BRITAIN had produced one of the great turn-of-the-century architect-designers, Charles Rennie Mackintosh, who was to have a profound influence on Continental design and on Modernism in general, the country as a whole was not keen to embrace the Glasgow School, nor the sympathetic, proto-modern design movement in Vienna. Barring the odd, occasional commission (more often than not entrusted to a foreigner), innovative contemporary design did not make its appearance in Britain until well into the 1920s. Before that time, vestigial Victorian and successive Edwardian interiors, all firmly rooted in tried-and-true taste, had been the staple in the country. Rumblings of dissatisfaction and change were heard in pre-1920s Britain, though, but these were usually from isolated, eccentric sources. The Omega Workshops, for instance, founded by Roger Fry (1866-1934), Duncan Grant (1885-1978) and Vanessa Bell (1879-1961), existed from 1913 to 1919, designing and decorating furniture, pottery, textiles, carpets and a few interiors in a joyful, colour-filled and highly distinctive manner.

Women were very much in the forefront of interior design in the 1910s and 1920s in Britain as in America, and the chic, though still somewhat tradition-bound, room settings by Syrie Maugham and Sibyl Colefax are worth a mention. Maugham's interiors were largely based on past styles, but her palette was bold and jaunty and produced interesting juxtapositions, such as antique red-lacquered furniture situated in a drawing room with pale yellow walls and drapes. But her most renowned interior was that of her own drawing room in the King's Road, Chelsea, the so-called 'all-white room' that she dramatically unveiled at midnight at a party in April 1927. Sibyl Colefax was proving strong competition for Maugham by 1930. A friend of Virginia Woolf, Colefax became a decorator after the Wall Street Crash, when she lost most of her assets (her grandfather had founded *The Economist*). Her style was very much in the pastel-pretty, Adamesque tradition, so appropriate to the English country house and its urban counterpart, and it proved extremely successful with her élite clientele (and continues to do so today, thanks largely to the firm of Colefax and Fowler, which still thrives).

Another British woman was also making a name for herself in the late 1920s in interior design, but, unlike Maugham and Colefax, Betty Joel (b.1896) looked elsewhere for her designs – forward, not back, and also to the Continent, Paris art and design of the mid-1920s not only influencing her own creations, but also being sold by her in her London showroom. Born Betty Lockhart in China, where her father was an administrator, and educated in England, she eventually married David Joel, an affluent South African, with whom she settled in London after World War I. Together they established a furniture manufactory in Portsmouth, with a showroom in London's Sloane Street. The simple, smart furniture which they sold – largely characterized by curved edges which Joel herself said reflected 'the Feminine form' – was sheathed in rich, often exotic wood veneer; offered for sale with these pieces were area rugs with abstract motifs, smart dressing-table mirrors and other modish accessories. When Joel opened her larger premises in the late 1920s in Knightsbridge, where some dozen model rooms were on view, she also displayed paintings by Marie Laurencin (her personal favourite), drawings by Raoul Dufy and Henri Matisse, Lalique light fixtures, rugs by Bruno da Silva Bruhns and also some carpets of her own design, hand-knotted in China. Although she was commissioned to design interiors for such eminent clients as Winston Churchill and Lord Mountbatten – and she created many an ultramasculine library and office for others – it was her primary aim to design 'for the working woman'. In accordance with this, her furniture designs were eminently comfortable and practical, with few corners to dust; likewise, her interiors sometimes featured veneered walls without right angles – just smooth, rounded surfaces that resembled many of the Streamline Moderne interiors of 1930s New York.

The modernity of E. Curtis Moffat (d.1942) and John Duncan Miller, whose interior designs are somewhat related, was not in fact so far removed from that of Betty Joel. Beautifully veneered furniture, with nicely rounded edges, was found in American-born Moffat's Fitzroy Square gallery (opened in 1929) and he, too, had a penchant for things French, offering for sale Evelyn Wyld rugs, Raymond Templier jewellery and Marie Laurencin paintings, among other domestic and foreign articles. The designer John Duncan Miller, one-time employee of Moffat and later owner of his own 'avant-garde' shop in London, along with his wife Madeleine, designed his own furniture as well as selling contemporary Parisian pieces, including designs by Eileen Gray.

Denham MacLaren (b.1903) was a one-time employee of furniture designer Arundell Clarke who provided some interesting furniture designs and room schemes to discerning English clients. In 1930 he opened a shop in Davies Street (later moving to Grosvenor Street), selling sturdy wood-veneered furniture – much of it nicely curved, like Betty Joel's – as well as more unconventional pieces, such as a glass-topped, painted-wood and chromium-plated metal-based occasional table that was strongly Modernist. Other London decorators – Hartigan Ltd., Bird Iles Ltd., Ronald Grierson, Maurice Adams and Derek Patmore – provided clients with Modernist or semi-Modernist interiors in the 1930s, but the most successful 'packagers' of such rooms were the esteemed firms of Heal and Son, Waring & Gillow, and Gordon Russell.

Although the furniture of Sir Ambrose Heal (1872-1959) is generally thought of as being in the updated, solid, Arts and Crafts vein, some pieces created in the 1930s (he was active in the firm until 1939) have a decidedly Modernist look, with strongly angular as well as smooth veneered and glass surfaces, zigzag-motif upholstery, tubular-metal frames (Mies van der Rohe chairs were sold through Heal's) and accessories such as geometric-patterned rugs and Moderne lighting fixtures being offered in Heal catalogues and showrooms to an eager public. Likewise, Sir Gordon Russell (1892-1980) was influenced by the forms and tenets of the Arts and Crafts Movement early in his furniture-designing career, but in around 1930 his style manifested a distinct Modernism, largely informed by the Bauhaus. Gordon Russell Ltd. offered a variety of furniture and accessories to the public, including geometric

Sir Gordon Russell's early furniture was produced in the Arts and Crafts mode, but around 1925 he introduced machine production into his Worcestershire factory and chic Modernist forms into his design repertoire.

rugs by the talented Marian Pepler, who was married to Gordon's brother, R.D. Russell.

Waring & Gillow, more so than Heal's and Gordon Russell, wholeheartedly embraced the forms of modern design, even of Parisian Art Deco. The original furniture-making firm of Robert Gillow, founded in the late seventeenth century in Lancaster, became known as Waring & Gillow in around 1900, after merging with S.J. Waring & Sons. The manufacturing and retail outlet's connection with Modernism was primarily due to the talents and wherewithal of one man, Serge Chermayeff (b.1900), the Russian-born architect-designer who married into the Waring & Gillow dynasty and subsequently became the director of its newly established Modern Art Studio (with which Paul Follot was also associated), a position he held from 1928 to 1931. He made use of tubular-metal forms, bright colours, built-in furniture systems, even luxuriant surfaces covering wood, such as a gold-leafed and lacquered cabinet of *c*. 1930, its front embellished with an incised stylized floral design. The interiors he designed for Waring & Gillow were the epitome of modern luxury, from an angular Australian walnut living-room suite, its upholstery awash in a pattern of triangles, to a similarly smart dining-room ensemble, its simple refectory table standing on a solitary piece of chromed-steel tubing, its veneered sideboard nicely architectonic and subtly patterned abstract carpets on the floor.

The interiors of architects Chermayeff, Wells Coates (1895-1958), Oliver Hill (1887-1968), Raymond McGrath (1903-1977), Brian O'Rorke (1901-1974) and David Pleydell-Bouverie (b.1911) best expressed the Modernist spirit emerging in Britain in the 1930s, with additional statements coming from the likes of architect Erich Mendelsohn, Hungarian-born architect-designer Marcel Breuer (who, like Walter Gropius, worked in Britain from 1934 to 1937) and even painter-designer Paul Nash (1889-1946), who designed a spectacular peach-coloured glass and mirror bathroom for dancer Tilly Losch in 1932. McGrath was an Australian-born architect who was deeply interested in glass in its many uses and permutations. Many of his domestic interiors featured a wealth of mirrored and other glass, including Finella, the Regency-era house of Cambridge University don Mansfield Forbes, which McGrath remodelled in 1929 (it was named after the mythical Celtic queen whose palace was made entirely of glass).

The largely do-it-yourself interiors put together using tubular-steel and other modern elements and even bent-wood furniture began to appear widely in British homes of the 1930s. The firm P.E.L. (Practical Equipment Ltd.), founded in London around 1931, produced smart sofas whose pitch-filled steel-tube frames curved at the corners, as well as countless chairs, tables, desks, bed frames, even bar stools and tea trolleys. Both Heal's and Waring &

This sleek early 1930s London interior, with its animal-skin rug and upholstery, tubular-metal table, architectonic corner cabinet and Moderne fire surround, was created by Bowman Brothers, a Camden Town firm.

Gillow marketed P.E.L. designs, and numerous designers employed them in their commissions, both private and public – among them Chermayeff, McGrath and Oliver P. Bernard, whose clients included the Strand Palace Hotel, biscuit-maker and tea-importer J. Lyons and Company (whose Corner Houses he designed) and Bakelite Ltd., the plastics manufacturer.

THE HIGHLY SIGNIFICANT IDEAS, designs and room ensembles of Peter Behrens and other members of the Deutscher Werkbund influenced the Modernist school of Parisian 1920s and 1930s design – and International Modernism in general – as did, to an extent, the designs of the Wiener Werkstätte in Austria. But there were several other designers working in these two countries whose styles differed considerably from their basically functionalist counterparts. Bruno Paul (1874-1968), for example, who studied at Dresden's school of applied arts and then worked at the Munich Academy and then the Berlin Kunstgewerbemuseum, was for some years associated with a traditional neo-classical style, a type that many wealthy, discerning clients wished to have their homes decorated in.

Dagobert Peche (1887-1923), who studied architecture in Vienna and was highly influenced by the French Rococo style, represented an exuberant, highly decorated strain of design within the Wiener Werkstätte, which he became associated with around 1915. Although he was not known for his room schemes (though one was shown at the 1913 Secession exhibition), Peche – who was also drawn to the Biedermeier style of the previous century – created lovely, highly ornamented ceramics, glassware, wallpaper, bookbindings and other accessories which gave Viennese design of the 1920s a new look, contrasting with the rectilinear designs of Hoffmann and Moser.

ALTHOUGH ITALY was very receptive to the Art Nouveau style, which was often referred to in that country as 'Stile Liberty', after the London retailer, Arthur Lasenby Liberty, it was not as sympathetic to Art Deco, and certainly not that high-style version which harked back to eighteenth-century French forms. There were, however, opulent interiors that could be said to be related to Art Deco – a c.1920 dining room by G.B. Gianotti of Milan, for instance, its vaguely neoclassical table and chairs decorated with stylized volutes, anthemions and other devices, or a c.1931 bedroom by Tomaso Buzzi, also of Milan, its blocky case furniture and more traditional slender-legged centre table lacquered in red.

The Milanese architect Gigiotti Zanini created interiors in the early 1930s which were opulent and grand, and contained some regular geometric patterns and even a sunburst motif (this one on a leaded demilune window in a bathroom). Other Milanese architects and designers were more Modernist in outlook (indeed that northern city was a hotbed of the applied arts, and from 1933 held a triennial exhibition devoted to them), including Franco Albini and Piero Portaluppi. Their interiors included built-in furniture elements, multiple-use pieces and interesting colour combinations. A dressing room of *c*.1933, designed by Albini for aviator Arturo Ferrarin's house, was as Streamline Moderne as any Kem Weber room in California: its walls were covered with brown and yellow striped silk, its sofa was upholstered in pink silk and its nicely curving dressing table, surmounted by a mirror as wide as it was tall, was partially lacquered in pink. An appropriate accessory was the big zebra-skin pillow lying on the sofa.

More comfortable yet practical Moderne interiors appeared in Italy, such as those by Gherardo Bosio of Florence, who preferred bright colours, built-in furniture, white walls and a smattering of geometric motifs. Perhaps the best-known Italian architect-designer of the century was another Milanese, Gio Ponti (1892-1979), who worked as a painter and ceramics designer in the 1920s (the latter for the Richard-Ginori factory in Doccia). He also designed a residence for Tony Bouilhet, head of the French goldsmith firm Christofle, in 1926, and served as director of the *triennale* applied-arts exhibition in Milan (it was originally conceived as a *biennale* in Monza). Ponti's interiors (like the hallway of his own house, Casa Ponti in Milan, dating from the mid-1930s) were elegant, airy and comfortable at the same time, not at all like the cold marble reception areas that greeted one all too often in grand Italian homes.

THE HIGHLY FUNCTIONAL, primary-coloured De Stijl interiors of Theo van Doesburg, Gerrit Rietveld and other rationally oriented, primarily Dutch architect-designers could not have been more at odds with the opulent, high-style confections by Ruhlmann and his contemporaries. Often short on comfort but rife with revolutionary ideas like movable partitions and multipurpose furniture, such dwellings as Rietveld's Schröder House in Utrecht, on which he closely collaborated with the owner, Mrs. Truus Schröder, proved fascinating if isolated essays in Dutch exterior-interior harmony. Felix Del Marle (1889-1952) was a French painter associated for a time with the De Stijl group; earlier he had supported the Italian Futurists. He eagerly adopted their forms and ideas, and in 1926 applied them to a living-room suite for a 'Madame B.' of Dresden.

There were of course other types of architecture and interior design that existed in Holland in the 1920s and 1930s, most of them more appealing at the time to the public than the rigorous, intellectual De Stijl. The Amsterdam School, led by Michel de Klerk (1884-1923), which flourished from approximately 1915 to 1930, was an avant-garde, expressionist group responsible for many single buildings in that city.

The Amsterdam School's idea of interior design – which they sometimes referred to as 'spatial design' – was a somewhat utopian-decorative one, revelling in ornamental detail, but not stinting on comfort and warmth (two very important elements of the Dutch interior, as that country's artists had shown for centuries in their interior scenes). Ideally, these spatial designs included components, both two- and three-dimensional, which were based on the same concept of design, thus together adding up to an architectural whole. One of De Klerk's suites was executed in 1916 for the retail store, 't Woonhuys, in somewhat sombre shades – dark woods, deep blue and violet carpet and wall-hanging – but it was imbued with an almost breathing, organic quality, coupled with a quasi-Oriental sense of mystery; there were even tassels and pillows galore, à la Paul Poiret's Ballets Russes-inspired settings.

THE 1920S AND 1930S in these far-northern European countries were not ground-breaking decades in terms of design, though certain figures – such as Alvar Aalto in Finland – did create furniture, objects and interiors that bespoke a familiarity with what was going on elsewhere in the contemporary design world, and even made significant statements of their own that made an impact elsewhere, especially in terms of subsequent decades, when Scandinavian design came to the fore.

The style that was already being called Swedish Modern in the 1930s began to take shape and assert itself in that country, with Denmark developing its own brand of Modernism as well. With no overt references to the past, stylishly modern, practical and unfussy rooms took form in accordance with this Scandinavian Modern idiom, its substance characterized, according to a contemporary American writer, by 'common sense shapes and colors, agreeable softness of contour and texture. Proportions are small, comfortable and familiar; light woods, muted values of clear colors, and a general air of reasonableness have made it a distinct, popular style for several years'.

In terms of domestic interiors, there were many architects and designers working in Scandinavia who were adherents of what can loosely be termed the International Modernist style, with echoes and elements of the Bauhaus, De Stijl, the Deutscher Werkbund and Le Corbusier to be seen in the simple, practical, well-made and basically functionalist components making up a home. A 1934 study designed by Danes Arne Jacobsen and Flemming Lassen, for instance (executed by N.C. Christofferson of Copenhagen), could be located anywhere on the Continent, and a contemporary description appended to a photograph of the room could refer to so many others of the 1930s: 'Comfort and convenience in the design of the armchairs and other fittings of the room have been a chief consideration'.

Eliel Saarinen had already left his native Finland by 1923, but Alvar Aalto (1898-1976) only started his architectural practice that year. Although his mid-1920s interiors were generally of a simple, cosy, quasi-classical nature, by 1929 his style was decidedly Modernist. His Paimio Sanatorium of 1929-33 included much moulded plywood (and laminated birchwood) seating, furniture types he was to improve upon and exploit for years, with international repercussions. He patented a process for bending wood in 1933 and other innovations – and much success – were to follow. Also in 1933 his furniture was shown outside Finland – at Fortnum & Mason in London – and soon he started up, along with his wife Aino and patron Maire Gullichsen, the firm Artek, in order to manufacture his furniture, light fittings and fabrics (as it continues to do today).

ALTHOUGH ON THE WHOLE Eastern Europe was impervious, whether by choice or economics, to the influence of modes of contemporary interior design emanating from the West (less so in terms of individual objects, such as ceramics and glass), there were the occasional manifestations of decorative *art moderne* or sturdy Modernism in these countries, sometimes filtered through or combined with regional idioms, materials or techniques, at times singularly distinctive, without any precedents or analogues elsewhere. Of course, these countries had exhibited at the 1925 Paris Exposition, and there were several strong statements made there in terms of interior design in these countries. Inside the Russian pavilion, for instance, the painter Rodchenko designed a workers' reading room – its high ceiling, light-painted walls, two-part slant-top reading table and twelve modified-tub chairs, their backs and two side rails extending all the way down to the floor, presented a clean, crisp Modernist setting, with more than a nod to the Deutscher Werkbund and Wiener Werkstätte. In fact, Le Corbusier, Mallet-Stevens and other French Modernists roundly admired the pavilion, whose architect was Konstantin Melnikov. This visionary architect also created an amazing building in Moscow in 1927: it was his own house, and it comprised two interconnecting brick cylinders covered with stucco. The rear cylinder was – and still is – one of the most astounding domestic structures in the world, honeycombed as it is with some five dozen elongated hexagonal windows. Whatever the original furnishings comprised – one *c.* 1930 photograph offers a glimpse of a simple work desk and bent-wood chair – the interior had to have been one of the wonders of Europe, especially on a sunny day, when light would have streamed in from nearly all directions, intersecting, conjoining, doubtless creating crazy patterns on the floor, ceiling and whatever else it touched.

In Czechoslovakia, Cubism was a strong influence on designers, and indeed whole rooms of Cubist-inspired furniture, glassware, metalwork and so on appeared as early as 1910-12. Architect-designer Pavel Janák was one of the premier exponents of this style, which also reflected contemporary Viennese design, and among his Cubist creations were covered boxes of stoneware glazed white, their multiangular forms – like prototypical geodesic domes – then outlined with black paint.

Hungary was the Eastern European country most receptive to Art Nouveau, its exotic, Oriental-Magyar roots complementing the joyful, organic, curvilinear forms of that style. Some two decades later, a few Hungarian designers promoted an opulent style somewhat akin to Parisian Art Deco, especially the feminine, pastel-hued style of Groult and Laurencin. For instance, a c.1934 bedroom designed by János Beutum of Budapest had slightly curving, but essentially rectilinear furniture lacquered in pale rose, and a plush carpet of black velour. On the wall Beutum, an architect, painted a mural depicting an ethereal landscape, dominated by a somewhat Orientalizing tower overlooking tree-tops and mountains.

Folk-art tradition often melded with elements of Moderne design in Eastern Europe, as in a Polish dining room of the 1920s, its solid wood table and chairs carved with stylized floral designs, these more akin to the naïve blossoms painted by the Omega Workshops in England than the more sophisticated bouquets that garnished many French Art Deco furniture pieces and interiors. Two rooms shown in the Polish pavilion of the 1925 Paris Exposition, however, are bereft of any organic elements. Mieczylas Kotarbinski's study-office, with its jutting angularity, is more aligned to Czech Cubism, whereas Adalbert Jastrzebowski's dining room is softer and gentler, the chair backs shaped like flattened hourglasses, the lower walls covered with batik mural hangings sporting cheerful floral designs (these were made by the Krakow Ateliers).

BOTH THE RICH, high-style strain of Art Deco and its more functionalist-Modernist contemporary could be found in private residences far from France. In most instances, these interiors were created by Frenchmen or other foreigners, but sometimes by native architects and designers who had been educated abroad – or visited Europe extensively.

In the somewhat surprising location of Tokyo, a superb Modernist house was erected in 1933 for Prince Yasuhiko Asaka and his family (his wife, Princess Nobuko, was the eighth daughter of the Emperor Meiji), its design in part attributed to the prince, who had a keen interest in modern architecture. He was also much taken with French design of the 1920s, having lived in Paris from 1922 to 1925 and visited the 1925 Exposition. The two-storey dwelling – which today houses the Tokyo Metropolitan Teien Art Museum – was designed by a group of workers from the Imperial Household Department, and its interiors were entrusted to Henri Rapin, the multitalented painter-designer who for a time was artistic director of the Sèvres porcelain factory. In addition, lighting fixtures and a glass-relief door were created for the house by René Lalique.

A pair of Indian rulers, the Maharajah of Indore and the Maharajah Sir Umaid Singh in Jodhpur, Rajasthan, both decided to have their palaces decorated in the new Moderne style in the late 1920s/early 1930s. Manik Bagh, or Temple of Rubies, was the young Prince Yeshwant Roa Holkar Bahadur's new Indore palace, located some 350 miles northeast of Bombay in present-day Madhya Pradesh. It was designed by Eckhart Muthesius, son of the Deutscher Werkbund figure, Hermann Muthesius, and it proved an architectural gem. The Maharajah of Jodhpur's palace, Umaid Bhawam (today in part a luxurious hotel), was furnished in a somewhat less avant-garde, more upper-class-London-opulent manner, as befitted its sumptuous Anglo-Indian setting.

Art Deco in Australia was, not surprisingly, largely indebted to British design of the 1920s and 1930s, mostly by way of Australian architects who had visited or studied in Europe (some also showed an American influence in their work). Harry Norris, for instance, who had been sent by his firm to observe shop design and construction in Europe and North America, was commissioned to create a three-storey domestic dwelling for the pharmaceuticals magnate Alfred Nicholas in the early 1930s. Burnham Beeches, as the house was called, was completed in 1933 in Sherbrooke, near Melbourne, and is considered the finest example of Art Deco in Australia (today it is a hotel).

Donald Deskey designed a private flat above Radio City Music Hall for its manager, 'Roxy' Rothafel. Its office (*below*), with high, gilded ceiling, panelled cherrywood walls and gleaming glass, metal and lacquered furniture and objects, provided an opulent setting for the impresario. Deskey has said that his design was influenced by the 1925 Paris Exposition, and indeed echoes of the elegant Modernism of Pierre Chareau or Michel Dufet can be seen, even down to the ingenious built-in furniture hidden by some of the wall panels. The Music Hall Women's Lounge (*right*) was decorated by Yasuo Kuniyoshi with murals of monumental flowers and leaves. Deskey's delicate chairs for the curved-wall room are reminiscent of forms by Ruhlmann and nicely complement the somewhat surreal tendrils and blossoms.

In 1933-34 Donald Deskey designed this elegant dining room (*left*) for the Manhattan apartment of Abby Rockefeller Milton. The glazed-silver walls and ceiling were offset by the richly grained Macassar ebony of the Gallic-inspired table and white-leather-covered chairs. Note the interesting lighting fixtures at the side of the round mirror and in the centre of the etched-mirror-topped table.

The designer of the amazing stepped bed dominating this publicity photograph of Hollywood actor Warren William (*below*) is not identified, but the piece – though not, alas, the entire room – is very much in the American skyscraper-Moderne style. Note the doors on the headboard that open to reveal cylindrical reading lamps.

Saks Fifth Avenue head Adam Gimbel was one of Donald Deskey's earliest clients, whose Park Avenue residence Deskey designed in 1927. Its study (*above*), conceived in shades of tan, yellow and brown, included custom-made furnishings of stainless steel and other metals, with corkboard walls, copper ceiling and linoleum floor. Some pieces first made for private commissions, such as the desk lamp on the left made up of three tiers of triangles, were later offered to the public by Deskey-Vollmer, Inc.

Gilbert Rohde designed furniture of chromed tubular metal, Bakelite, wood and wicker in an atelier he set up in New York in 1929, and by the 1930s he was exhibiting and being commissioned to create whole interiors including his own and others' pieces. The attractive, earth-toned 'Piano Room' and 'Library' (*left* and *below*) shown here date from the mid 1930s and illustrate Rohde's interest in comfort, taste and modernity. Many of his space-saving designs were mass-produced by major furniture-making firms in the American Midwest.

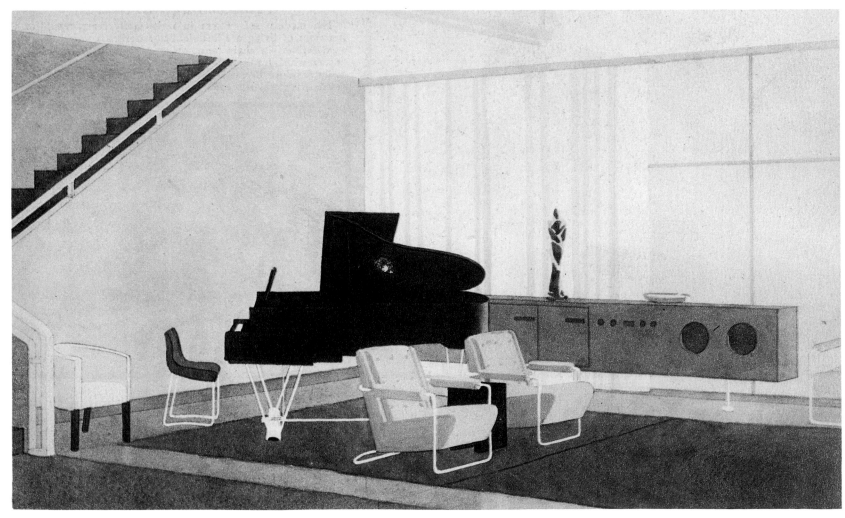

This bathroom (*right*) appeared in a 1930 design magazine and is quite an elegant space, from the series of arcs on the window and panel on the right, to the elegant gilded legs on the blue sink and the *curule*-type stool in front of it. The inset shelves and drawers to the right of the sink lend a practical touch, but the figure bearing the illuminated sphere is clumsy.

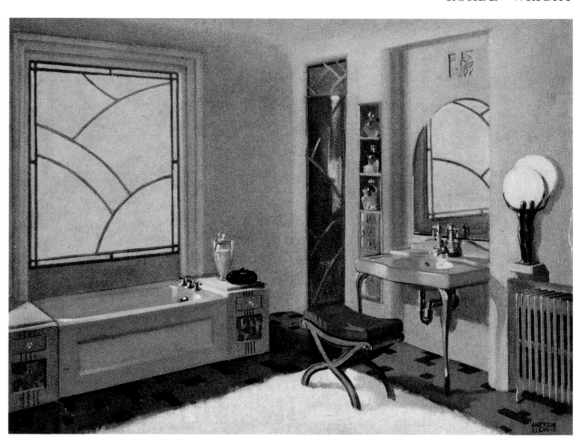

Russel Wright, who believed that 'good design was for everyone', went into business in 1927, designing fabrics, china and flatware, among other things. He created versatile furniture for Heywood-Wakefield and made extensive use of metal in both his objects and interior schemes. The 1933 living room (*below*), with its light-green walls and blue and brown furniture, is punctuated by the gleaming copper of the lamps, occasional table, vases and fire.

Paul T. Frankl was an American success story, creating some of New York's most exuberant and luxurious Moderne furniture and interiors. Among his designs were skyscraper bookcases and cabinets, such as the one in the 1929 living room (*below*), their stepped silhouettes echoing those of Manhattan's ever-rising edifices. He was also inspired by the Orient (which he had visited), with pieces or whole rooms lacquered, gilt or silvered in the Eastern manner, or with pierced openwork and forms in the Chinese style, such as the low, mirror-topped coffee table in the same living room and in the 1935 room (*opposite right*). The late 1920s half-moon desk, triangular chair and tasselled mirror (*opposite left*) were finished with bright Chinese-red lacquer and black trim.

New York decorator Harriet E. Brewer created this elegant space (*above*) c. 1930. It contained *de rigueur* Manhattan-Moderne components: a skyscraper-style bookcase-cabinet, a screen and carpet with modish abstract motifs. The maple and chromium-plated metal furniture (and the conical-shaded lamp) were by Russian-born Alexander Kachinsky.

Eliel Saarinen was another émigré to the United States who found much success in his new home, in this case Michigan's Cranbrook Academy of Art. His early designs in Finland were firmly rooted in the light and/or painted woods and simple yet elegant forms of Germany and Scandinavia, and his subsequent American furniture and interiors developed this basic aesthetic further, often assuming decorative characteristics gleaned from Paris or Vienna. The dining room in the president's house at Cranbrook (*above*), with its light-wood-veneered table and chairs highlighted with vertical fillets of black, is as harmonious an ensemble as any Parisian room setting, and his tiled bathroom (*opposite*) is a stark but stunning essay on the vertical and horizontal.

Raymond Loewy and John Vassos were well-known New York industrial designers who created interiors as well as objects. Vassos designed an attractive and practical studio for photographer Margaret Bourke-White (*above*), its built-in components, according to a 1933 journal, 'as conveniently and economically planned as those in a ship's cabin'. For his own Manhattan penthouse, Loewy designed simple but dramatic spaces: the entrance lobby (*right*) featured a black linoleum floor, yellow walls and grey-painted furniture with chromium trim, while the living room (*above right*), with two oyster-white and two gold walls, was centred on an unusual white-painted fireplace.

The spacious lounge of Chicago's 1929 **Powhatan apartments** (*right*) was an inviting, sophisticated public space in an urban living complex, with its plush barrel chairs, jaunty end tables and ash-stands, and stylized mural of a noble Native American hunting deer. Note the geometric patterns on the ceiling's light panels, as well as on the mouldings, grilles and pelmet. (The building's architects were Robert S. Degolyer and Charles L. Morgan.)

Versatile industrial designer Walter Dorwin Teague, known for his camera, glassware, car and cash register designs, also created interiors, such as this late 1930s lounge (*below*) for La Société Matford, Paris. Warm, white walls emerged from a wainscot with narrow silvered strips, boxy chairs were covered in white, light grey-green and coral leather, and the long centre and side tables, as well as the fireplace and chimney, were sheathed in mirror-glass.

Betty Joel's primary aim was to design 'for the working woman', but that did not mean her furniture and interiors were exclusively for a female clientele. The 1938 study her firm created for Lord Mountbatten's London home (*left*) was cosy, comfortable and practical. An ice-blue relief map of the world dominated the wall, and some of the furniture was painted the same hue. The natural-cedar centre table, with solid-glass legs, has a top protected by glass, as does a shelf attached to a sofa. Light-wood furniture and a similarly light palette dominate Joel's living room (*below*), whose natural-oak furniture, but for the centre tables, assumes quite traditional forms. The walls and ceiling are cream-coloured, the geometric area rug pastel-hued and the upholstery, wall lights and overmantel vase provide orange highlights.

Of light wood and subtle curves, this efficient workroom-study (*right*) was designed by Rodney Thomas for Ashley Havinden *c.* 1933. Note especially the large Modernist clock affixed to the wall, its colours reflected on the BP poster on the right.

Betty Joel's pine-walled sitting room (*below*) was more colourful than the sitting room opposite; it had a curved-edge divan and bright abstract carpets.

Betty Joel, Ltd., designed this doctor's consulting room (*left*) *c.* 1931, along with architect A.B. Llewellyn Roberts. The sleekly curvilinear desk and other furniture were of Queensland silky oak and Monel metal.

These two mid-1930s bedrooms, the one (*above*) designed by Betty Joel for the Royal Academy Exhibition of British Art in Industry (and appearing in one of her advertisements), the other by London designer John Duncan Miller (*right*), are both distinguished for their nicely curved forms – Joel's room (or rather its one wall) is curved as well – and the use of figured veneer. Miller's dressing table and chair are especially attractive, with their parabolic silhouettes.

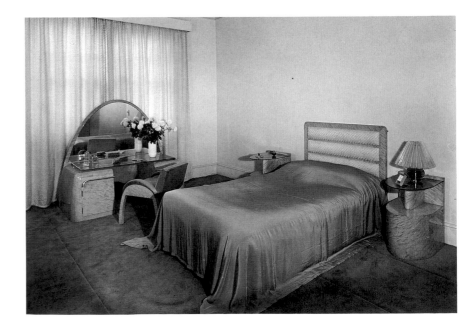

Though largely tradition-bound, some of the interiors of London decorator Syrie Maugham had Modernist overtones. The drawing room of her own King's Road home, unveiled in 1927, was a symphony of whites and creams, including the beige-satin covers of the settees, the off-white Louis Quinze chairs, the cut flowers and the huge Marion Dorn rug. Abundant mirrors and discreet, indirect lighting contributed to the overall drama and purity of the room, which is said to have begun a craze for all-white décor.

This early 1930s model room (*left*) was designed for the General Electric Company in order to enlighten the public as to the types of direct and indirect illumination available. The cornice lights at the top of the walls are especially dramatic, and the engraved mirror and silver-painted table, chairs and fireplace further heighten the apple-green room.

The London decorating firm of Bird Iles Ltd. created this bright, comfortable, harmonious living room (*left*) in 1937. The pale walls are punctuated by copper lamps, and the polished-cork floor blends nicely with the Australian silky-oak furniture. Tomato-red highlights appear on a pillow and on area rugs, and turquoise tweed upholstery provides a fitting foil to the room's dominant earthy tones.

Russian-born architect-designer Serge Chermayeff made extensive use of tubular-metal forms, bright colours, built-in furniture systems and sometimes luxurious surfaces in his room schemes. The *c.* 1930 showroom for a British dressmaking firm (*left*) has silver-grey backgrounds, carpet-covered rubber floors, and black-and mirrored-glass wall panels. The tubular-copper, yellow-covered chairs provide a sunny spot of colour in a bright, sky-lighted space dominated by neutral shades.

In the early 1930s, Serge Chermayeff designed a handsome, practical living room-cum-studio for the sculptor A.G. Gibbons Grinling (*below*). The wall panels are of Australian walnut, the long studio windows draped in jute, and most of the furniture is built in, with ample space for sculptures.

Heal & Son was one of the most successful British packagers of Modernist interiors. Although the furniture of Sir Ambrose Heal is generally considered to be in an updated Arts and Crafts vein, many 1930s ensembles had a strong Modernist look, with zigzag-motif upholstery, tubular-metal frames, and accessories like geometric-patterned rugs and Moderne lighting fixtures. The dining room (*below*) is sleek and sophisticated, with *curule*-type chairs and matching table (of oval section chromium-plated steel tube), a black cellulose-enamelled sideboard, handsome glass- and metalware. The sturdy, largely rectilinear dining ensemble (*left*) is not without charm – and contemporary touches, such as the bold-patterned area rug and three-tiered wall lights. The bedrooms (*opposite*) are dominated by tubular metal, both curvilinear and rectilinear. The fabric hangings behind the beds add a welcome pattern to an otherwise austere room.

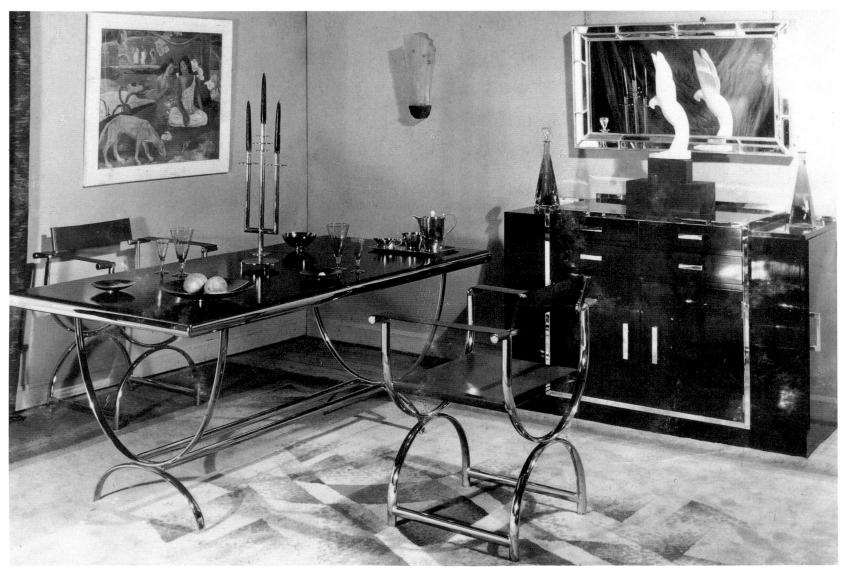

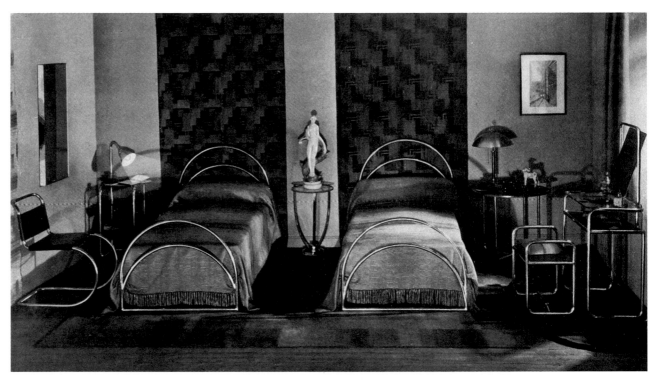

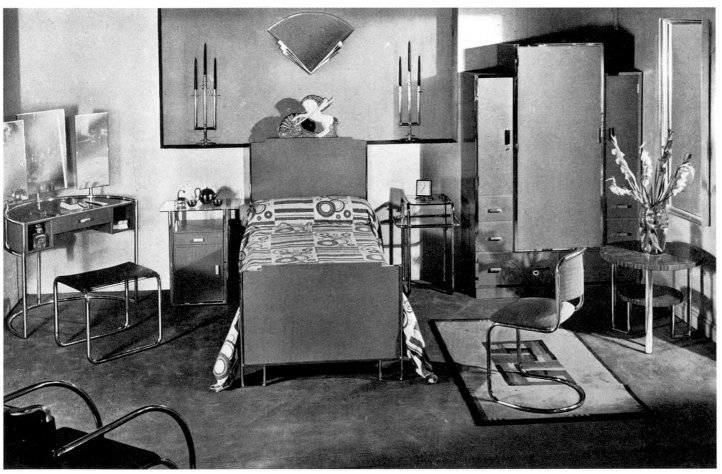

Images of antique Rome adorn the walls in this corner of Gordon Selfridge, Jr.'s, London sitting room (*left*), an opulent yet snug space. Note how the veining of the marble fireplace echoes the pattern of the animal skin covering the plush, built-in sofa; René Lalique's 'Tourbillons' vase can be seen under the wall light on the right.

This sophisticated 1930s London dining room (*below left*) has an interesting rectangle of ceiling light, and handsome rectilinear-Moderne furniture of both light and dark wood. The contemporary glass figurines nicely complement the painting of the classical nude over the bold fireplace.

The Modernist spirit emerging in 1930s Britain was expressed in interiors by architects such as Wells Coates. Although mainly a designer of shops, offices and other public spaces, he created several notable domestic interiors, including that of his own London flat in Yeoman's Row (*below*) in 1935. The spacious studio (on the top floor of an earlier building) is characterized by a great deal of light, P.E.L. tubular-steel and built-in furniture (there was also a loft bed), and a strong, even somewhat austere, sense of economy.

'New Ways' was toy-maker W. J. Bassett-Lowke's 1926 Northampton house, some of whose interiors were by German architect Peter Behrens (C.R. Mackintosh had designed rooms for the same client a decade earlier). The Behrens-designed, Deutscher Werkbund-influenced lounge (*right*) featured a blocky mantelpiece by the Allied Arts and Crafts Guild of Birmingham, some Mackintosh furniture and, somewhat surprisingly, a lively floral carpet from the Parisian atelier Primavera.

The dramatic hearth in this photograph (*below*) is English; designed in the late 1920s by C.A. Richter, it was produced by the Bath Cabinet Makers Co.

English furniture-making firm Hampton & Sons jumped on the Moderne bandwagon in the 1930s, adding smart streamlined and boxy pieces to their inventory (*below right*).

The best-known Italian designer of the twentieth century was Gio Ponti, who worked as a painter and ceramics designer in the 1920s and also founded the design journal *Domus*. The hallway of his mid-1930s Milan house (*opposite*) was dominated by a plush, green-covered banquette.

In the northern Italian lake city of Como, Gianni Mantero designed a lounge (*right*) for the Canottieri Lario Rowing Club. Its dominant Moderne element was a stylish mural by A. Songa. Black and white mosaics paved the floor, and the walnut furniture was low to the ground, with groups of the sturdy chairs and stools covered in various patterns.

A boldly Modernist interior was created *c*. 1931 by Alfio Fallica in Rome (*below*). The ultra-Moderne furniture of cypress, ebony, morocco leather and silvered metal included a low round table and two plump stools. Hugging the wall was a day-bed, over which was a decorative panel painted with a contented Europa astride the back of Zeus-as-bull.

Milanese architect Franco Albini designed Modernist rooms with built-in furniture and interesting colour combinations. The *c*. 1933 dressing room (*below right*) was for aviator Arturo Ferrarin and was as Streamline Moderne as a Kem Weber interior in California. Its walls were covered with brown and yellow striped silk, its sofa upholstered in pink silk and its dressing table partly lacquered in pink.

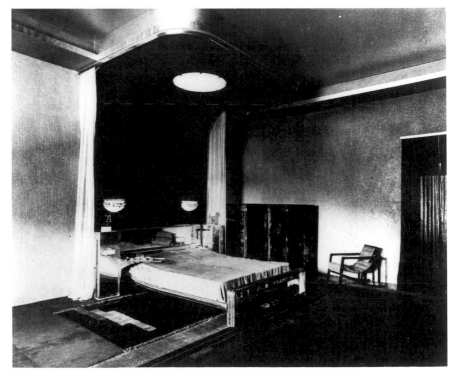

Manik Bagh, or the Temple of Rubies, was the palace belonging to the young Maharajah of Indore, whose architect, the ruler's Oxford friend, Eckhart Muthesius, spent much of 1930-33 creating an architectural gem with Modernist interiors in present-day Madhya Pradesh, some 350 miles northeast of Bombay. The photograph (*opposite below right*) shows the Maharajah's bedroom, with its aluminium and chromed-metal bed designed by Louis Sognot and Charlotte Alix and the brown-leather, lacquered wood and chromed-metal 'Transat' chair (*opposite below left*) by Eileen Gray. The colour photograph (*opposite left*) shows the bed in a somewhat altered, later setting, the 'Transat' having been replaced by Le Corbusier and Charlotte Perriand's chaise-longue (*opposite right*) (the leopard-skin cover is not original). On the right in the photograph is Muthesius's standard lamp with two red-painted bands echoing the metal shade; it is made of alpaca, a type of nickel silver of which the glass and metal appliques over the bed are also fabricated.

Examples of the Maharajah's furniture can be seen in these photographs; they were among over 200 works from his palace auctioned by Sotheby's Monaco in 1980. The office furniture (*below*) was designed by a thoroughly modern Ruhlmann and comprised a huge demilune desk, chairs and other pieces with chromed-metal fittings and mounts, Macassar ebony veneer and red-leather upholstery. The red armchair by Muthesius (*right*), one of a pair in the palace's library, stands on 'ski' feet of alpaca; reading lights are set into the upper side panels and a silver ashtray is embedded in the right arm. The dramatic green-glass and chromed-metal bed by Louis Sognot (*above right*) came from the Maharani's bedroom. (See overleaf for period black-and-white photographs of these and other pieces *in situ*.)

The **yellow and silver hall** in Manik Bagh (*opposite far left*) featured two boldly patterned da Silva Bruhns rugs on the floor and a ceiling comprising bits of sparkling glass; the seating was relatively simple but comfortable. On the wall hung a portrait of the Maharajah's father in a dandified pose. The gleaming office (*opposite below*) shows Ruhlmann's desk and chairs (see previous page), as well as a brown-leather-covered chair.

The **polished aluminium and chromed-metal bed** (*below right*) created by Louis Sognot and Charlotte Alix for the Maharajah's bedroom is shown here as illustrated in the 1933 edition of *The Studio Year Book of Decorative Art*.

The **focal point of the Maharani's bedroom** (*right*) was the green-glass and chromed-metal bed by Louis Sognot (see previous page), probably a collaborative effort with Charlotte Alix. Protective mosquito netting (here drawn to the wall) could be pulled round the bed at night.

The **palace's austere and formal dining room** (*below*) was illuminated by alpaca standard lamps by Muthesius, whose massive table was surrounded by thirty simple armchairs.

The **glass-doored library of Manik Bagh** (*left*), with furniture by Eckhart Muthesius, included a pair of red-leather armchairs (see previous page) surrounding a four-tiered round table of wood, alpaca and glass. Note the unusual wall light on the right; its background was painted cream, its dual-parallel-line border red.

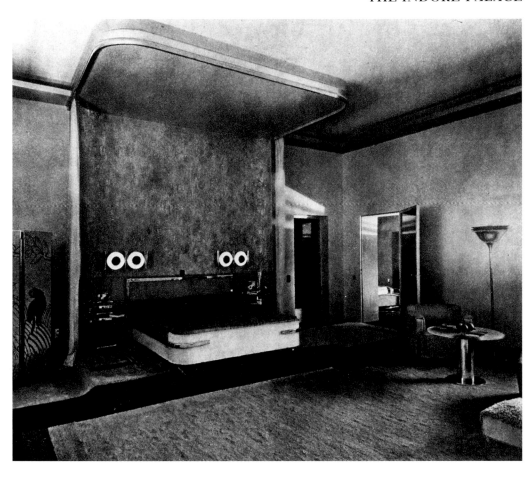

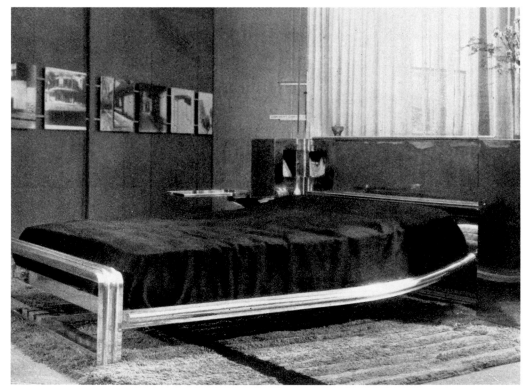

The Netherland Plaza Hotel, Cincinnati, (originally built in 1931) has been recently restored

CHAPTER 5

ART DECO IN PUBLIC PLACES
TRANSPORT, THEATRES AND CINEMAS, STORES, HOTELS, BARS AND OFFICES

Art Deco in all its best-known splendour appeared not in private homes or even temporary exhibitions, but in vast public spaces, such as cinemas and theatres, skyscrapers and hotel lobbies, restaurants and bars, even a few churches and schools. Most of these interiors appeared not in 1910s and 1920s Paris, where Art Deco was born, but in other countries in the late 1920s and 1930s, most especially the United States, where the interiors of Manhattan's towering skyscrapers vied with their decorative façades and ziggurat silhouettes in terms of rich, exuberant stylization, and where the sumptuous interior grandeur of the ubiquitous movie house was every bit as exotic as the magical black-and-white images flickering on the silver screen. The Hollywood sets themselves were a form of glittering Art Deco interior that dazzled the everyday moviegoer at home and abroad, and sometimes even inspired – in however small a way – the everyday 1930s interior. New (and sometimes merely improved) forms of transportation provided designers with excuses for creating Art Deco interiors, from the inner spaces of the actual vehicles themselves (railroad cars, aeroplanes and of course ocean liners), to the massive waiting rooms, lounges and bars of train stations and airport terminals.

NOT ONLY WERE the exteriors of trains, aircraft and automobiles designed in the Streamline Moderne vein, but their interiors also featured Modernist elements. Likewise, the many large buildings, such as railroad terminals and airports, that were erected in connection with land and air travel at times contained outstanding Art Deco interiors, many decorated with huge murals or sculptures relating to speed and transportation.

Air travel, of course, was a child of the twentieth century, and it is not surprising to discover that aircraft in the 1920s and 1930s displayed Art Deco touches. René Joubert and Philippe Petit of the Paris design firm D.I.M., for instance, designed a chic passenger section for a Farman aeroplane prior to 1925 (brothers Henri and Maurice Farman of Billancourt, France, were well-known aviators and aeroplane designers). The ill-fated German airship 'LZ 129 (Hindenburg)' was equipped with a smartly outfitted smoking room designed by Fritz August Breuhaus de Groot, its swivel-seated, leather-covered armchairs and matching square-top tables ranged around a space whose walls were decorated with the elliptical images of zeppelins. Britain's 'R100' airship of 1929, on the other hand, made extensive use of woven cane furniture, which was handsome as well as light-weight and practical.

Rail transportation was of course far more common than air in the 1920s and 1930s, and the interiors of some of the Pullman cars in Europe, especially France, were plush and opulent. René Lalique created glass-embellished interiors for several French trains, including the sleeping car of the French President in 1923 and Pullman cars on the opulent *Côte d'Azur* train in 1929.

In Britain, trains tended to the tubular-steel Modernist rather than decorative-plush style, although the 1937 LNER *Coronation* featured over-stuffed seats covered with a handsome chevron upholstery in the First Class car, and rounded tub chairs, and elaborate light fixtures and mouldings in the observation car. London Underground stations built in the 1930s were especially Modernist in their chromed-metal and all-curving guises, for instance, the cylindrical brick-faced Arnos Grove station on the Piccadilly Line (Adams, Holden & Pearson, 1931-34). Charles Holden was the principal designer of this project, as well as the Leicester Square tube station (1935) and the Park Royal tube station – all bright, gleaming geometric essays on the circle and square.

Several railroad terminals in the United States were outstanding examples of Art Deco architecture both inside and out, foremost among them the Cincinnati Union Terminal (Roland Anthony Wank of Fellheimer & Wagner) of 1929-33, a massive stepped and domed stone structure. Omaha's Union Station (Gilbert S. Underwood, 1929-31) was a more rectilinear, traditional structure, but its main waiting room manifested an array of Moderne components, from the huge chandeliers (resembling Ruhlmann's massive tiered *lustres* from afar, but in reality modern confections of tubular lights) to the geometric patterns on the floor, overdoor panels and upper walls.

Paul Philippe Cret, mastermind of the Cincinnati station's interior, also designed the interiors of over fifty railroad cars for Philadelphia's Edward G. Budd Company. Other notables lent their talents to designing Modernist Pullman, dining, smoking and observation cars, including Raymond Loewy and Norman Bel Geddes. The anonymous designer of the Santa Fe Railway's Acoma Super Chief created a Streamlined-Moderne-cum-Aztec setting in 1937 for the train's lounge, which was sheathed in rich veneers and dominated by a panel over the bar representing a stylized feather-bedecked Indian. On the other hand, Loewy's bar car of c.1938 for the Pennsylvania Railroad's *Broadway Limited* was a simple and soothing streamlined essay in shiny metal and shades of cream and grey.

THE 1920s AND 1930s French *paquebots*, or ocean liners, have often been referred to as the final triumph of Art Deco and indeed those massive vessels built by the Compagnie Générale Transatlantique, which commissioned Paris's premier designers to furnish them, can rightly be termed 'floating palaces' in a glittering era. Without doubt, the CGT's *Normandie* (1932-35) and earlier *Ile-de-France* (1927), successors to the French Line's *France* (1912) and *Paris* (1921), were the most spectacularly outfitted ships sailing the sea, though other countries whose lines plied the Atlantic and other waterways produced impressive vessels as well.

The *Ile-de-France* made her maiden voyage in 1926, the first major ocean liner to be launched after World War I. The very image of chic modernity – and coming hot on the heels of the 1925 Paris Exposition – the *Ile-de-France* proved a worthy ambassador for her country and the *années folles* of an affluent Europe. The *Paris* had originally been launched in 1921, but its interiors were given a Moderne facelift in 1929, keeping some elements, however, like Edgar Brandt's wrought-ironwork on balustrades and staircases. Rooms were designed by such notable figures as Léon Jallot, René Prou, René Lalique, Paul Follot, Süe et Mare, Maurice Dufrêne and Michel Dufet, with one of the chief transformations in many of them, especially the public spaces, being the replacement of heavy wood panelling with glass, mirrored or otherwise. Even the tearoom floor was recovered with illuminated glass.

But the Compagnie Générale Transatlantique's shining star was without doubt the *Normandie*, whose construction began in 1929 and which was launched from Le Havre, bound for New York harbour, on 29 May 1935. Its huge (and air-conditioned) public rooms shimmered and glistened with mirrored and plain glass, gold and silver leaf, and artificial light flooding in from massive ceiling, wall and other light fixtures. The Grand Salon and the *salle à manger*, or dining hall, in the First Class section were the most glittering spaces of all. The Grand Salon, the biggest public room ever built for an ocean-going vessel, was dominated by a four-part allegorical mural by Jean Dupas (1882-1964) occupying its four large corner wall sections. The Smoking Room was the creation of Jean Dunand, who had also been responsible for a handsome *fumoir* in the Ambassade Française at the 1925 Paris Exposition. The First Class Dining Room was a latter-day Galerie des Glaces, 305 feet (86 metres) long (13 metres longer than Versailles' gallery), 46 feet (13 metres) wide and 25 feet (9.5 metres) high. At the entrance one was greeted by two massive bas-relief gilt-stucco panels on the walls, one by Raymond Delamarre representing *Les Arts et les Monuments Normands*, the other *Les Sports et les Jeux* by Léon Drivier. Other reliefs, also depicting life in Normandy, were at the opposite end of the room, seemingly a city-block's length away, and presided over by *La Paix*, a gilt-bronze allegorical statue by Louis Dejean.

De luxe private quarters on the *Normandie* were created by famous designers, among them the 'Deauville' suite, by Louis Süe, with elegant, feminine, pinkish-white walls, a grand piano and other furniture of creamy burl ash (some chairs sported modified Louis Seize forms), and a gilt-bronze bas-relief of a reclining female nude by Albert Pommier. Jules Leleu's 'Trouville' suite was a more sombre creation, with dark-lacquered furniture and carpets with abstract designs by da Silva Bruhns. More Moderne was Dominique's 'Rouen' suite, whose salon walls were lacquered and covered with pigskin, with furniture veneered in Macassar ebony.

The *Normandie*, shining star of the French Line, contained several *de luxe* private quarters, among them the 'Deauville' suite by Louis Süe. Pink and white walls, a grand piano and various refined touches made its sitting room a most elegant, sublime floating refuge.

The Cunard-White Star liner, the *Queen Mary*, was launched in 1936, a monumental vessel intended to rival the *Normandie* and not without some wonderful Modernist touches, a few seemingly outright imitations of elements on the French ship. The Main Lounge, for instance, included carpeting covered with huge stylized blossoms and leaves, an overmantel rendering of unicorns caught in battle and huge alabaster urns lit from within; not exact replicas of Jean Dupas's murals and Maurice Daurat's huge pewter vases on the *Normandie*, but enough of a tribute to Paris nevertheless.

DURING THE DECADES in which Art Deco flourished, so did the nascent form of art and entertainment known as the movies. Mesmerizing moving images of black and white embellished big screens the world over – from Paris to Shanghai, London to Chicago, Amsterdam to Sydney – and more often than not the structures purpose-built to contain a film's eager audiences were as dazzling as the movies themselves, and unlike them, they were awash with three-dimensional colour, glitter and splendour. There were also the legitimate theatres – for revues, drama, music – built in the 1920s and 1930s and, for the wealthy who preferred another form of entertainment, several casinos in the *de luxe* style were designed (including American millionaire Frank Jay Gould's gleamingly opulent gambling premises on the Riviera, and Manhattan's Central Park Casino, designed by Joseph Urban).

In Paris, several outstanding theatres and cinemas were built in the 1920s and 1930s, although few of the latter in the rich, highly 'theatrical' style of London's Odeons and America's myriad 'movie palaces'. Some were elegant and relatively subtly embellished; for instance, Georges Gumpel's Théâtre de l'Alhambra cinema of *c*.1927, its lobby's ceiling awhirl with a design of overlapping circles, its floors covered with bold geometric patterns and rattan furniture all around the mezzanine lobby, and Pierre Patout's cinema, Théâtre Nouvel Immeuble Pleyel (destroyed by fire in 1928). Others boasted grand, large-scale interiors every bit as splendid and opulent as smaller grand salons. Arguably the most splendid such theatre was the Théâtre Daunou, designed by Armand-Albert Rateau in collaboration with Paul Plumet and Rateau's faithful client, couturière Jeanne Lanvin (the architect was Bluysen). This small jewel of a theatre, which opened in 1922, glittered like a sapphire – almost literally, since it was decorated primarily in blue, in a shade more accurately akin to the hue of cornflowers and so identified with the theatre's owner that it was called 'Bleu Lanvin'.

Emile-Jacques Ruhlmann also designed both a theatre and a cinema in Paris in the 1920s. The Théâtre de la Michodière, whose architect was Bruynell, opened in late 1925. The Cinéma Marignan in the Champs-Elysées (Bruynell was also its architect and it opened *c*.1928) featured a more elaborate

The washroom in the 52nd-storey executive suite of Manhattan's Chanin Building is dominated by cream, gold and green tiles. Among its salient features are the sunburst over engraved-glass shower doors, a recessed ceiling, gold-plated taps, and a row of avian tiles over the bath (hiding a ventilating duct). Jacques Delamarre was in charge of the overall interior decoration of the 1929 skyscraper.

The ceiling of the Marseilles Opéra (1927) foyer painted by Henri de Groux with grand mythological scenes; much of the wood- and plasterwork is in the traditional Neoclassical vein, but there are numerous *art moderne* touches. Among these are the wall lights, attached to mirrors surmounted by classical masks, and an array of stylized volutes, the most Moderne of gleaming openwork on the convex balustrades over the doorways Edgar Brandt. The interior of the Marseilles Opéra continues the Neoclassical theme of its foyer, but again in a stylized contemporary manner. The pillars, fountain and smoky tendrils painted on the fire curtain are especially attractive.

decorative scheme, with curtains, walls and openwork pediment covered with the same floral design (gilded and patinated, and similar to the fancy motif appearing on the walls of the Grand Salon in the Hôtel du Collectionneur).

Elsewhere on the Continent, theatres and cinemas in both ornate and purist guises appeared. One of the finest was the Tuschinski Theatre in Amsterdam (now a Cannon cinema), created and furnished in 1918-21 by various members of the Amsterdam School as a flamboyant but nonetheless harmonious mixture of architectural and design elements. From the colourful painted ceiling and carpeted floor in the lobby (these by J. Gidding), to its elaborate light fittings throughout, the Tuschinski remains a visionary, expressionistic 1920s setting.

Great Britain's Odeons, Granadas and other so-called 'palaces of entertainment', which grew up like so many giant gilded lilies in the 1930s, sported arguably the most glorious cinema interiors in Europe. Interiors could be of the elegant, graduated pastel-hued Streamline Moderne variety – like the Muswell Hill Odeon (well maintained today) and the Woolwich Odeon – or they could be baroque extravaganzas, like the Tooting Granada (1931; conceived as a neo-Gothic cathedral by its creator, Theodore Komisarjevsky), or the Gaumont State in Kilburn, George Coles's 1937 begilt, bemarbled and bejewelled *palais*.

Dozens of Odeons were indeed fine examples of what was essentially highly functional, mass-produced architecture built in record time, but the handsomest cinemas in Britain were the unique, custom-built ones, usually located in the larger metropolises. London's New Victoria Cinema was one of these, designed by W. E. Trent and E. Wamsley Lewis for Provincial Cinematograph Theatres, Ltd., in 1929-30 (today it is a legitimate theatre, the Apollo Victoria).

London's legitimate theatres of the time were not embellished as luxuriously – or indeed as outrageously – as some of the city's cinemas, but several memorable interiors were created by respected architects or designers in contemporary veins. Serge Chermayeff's Cambridge Theatre (its architects were Wimperis, Simpson and Guthrie) dates from 1929-30. Its foyer featured a geometric motif of circles and half-circles, on the flooring, the auditorium doors, mirrors and carpeting, while its curved interior was opulently sheathed in different shades of gold leaf, the darkest being the farthest from the proscenium arch. The Savoy Theatre, redecorated by Basil Ionides in 1929 (he was also responsible for reoutfitting the adjacent Savoy Hotel and Claridge's a bit earlier), was also embellished with varying shades of metallic leaf (in this case, silver lacquered to resemble gold), here throughout the auditorium (destroyed by fire in 1990), from the fluted walls under and about the balconies, to the recessed bas-relief panels covering the proscenium arch, each representing designs associated with the history of the area. The upholstery on the seats and the curtain was of earthy tones: beige, coral, rust.

The interiors of the myriad movie theatres of North America were arguably the most sparkling examples of the genre ever created – appropriately so for the nascent hub of the movie industry, which grew by dizzy leaps and bounds in the 1920s and 1930s. Luckily, a number of these 'movie palaces' have been preserved in their original splendour, or painstakingly restored to it, such as the Wiltern and Pantages theatres in Los Angeles, the Paramount in Aurora, Illinois, and the Pickwick in the nearby Chicago suburb of Park Ridge, and of course Manhattan's superb Radio City Music Hall.

Noted American cinema designers, who specialized in creating both the exteriors and interiors of these 'palaces of entertainment', were Timothy L. Pflueger (of the San Francisco architectural firm Miller & Pflueger), S. Charles Lee, B. Marcus Priteca and John Eberson, but many other notables – including Joseph Urban and Winold Reiss – also made significant contributions to cinema design. Theme cinemas, whose décors often fancifully reflected a native or exotic, past or present nation or culture, abounded, and such interiors – in the Aztec/Mayan, American Indian, Ancient Egyptian, Italian Renaissance or Baroque, Spanish Colonial or Chinese styles – were often accompanied by standard Art Deco-style fixtures.

In Los Angeles, the home base of the film industry, were the Pantages and Wiltern theatres, two of America's showiest, 'glitziest' cinemas. Los Angeles-based S. Charles Lee was responsible for the aluminium-fronted Wiltern (1929-31; originally called the Warner Bros. Western Theater), located on Wilshire Boulevard; inside members of the audience were enveloped and bedazzled by a veritable galaxy of Art Deco. Priteca's Pantages Theater (1929-30), on Hollywood Boulevard, was even more dazzling, with its busy fretwork of sunrays and scrolls surrounding a massive bronze and frosted-glass chandelier, billowing clouds and a flock of flying birds painted on the proscenium fire-curtain, and on the central of three panels over the stage a sleek androgynous Apollo leading his snorting steeds.

In the American Midwest, cinemas like the Fox Detroit Theater, the Colony Theater in Cleveland, and the Illinois establishments, the Paramount in Aurora and Pickwick in Park Ridge, were designed with outstanding streamlined-elegant or exotic-over-the-top interiors that were aeons away from the vast expanses of cornfields or urban sprawl the audiences lived with in the outside world. John Eberson, the Austrian-born, New York-based architect who co-created the Rex cinema in Paris in 1932, toned down and streamlined his style considerably five years later when he created Cleveland's Colony, interior spaces of which provided broad dramatic sweeps of soothing neutral and earthy tones (much like those used in the streamlined Odeons in Britain).

The mezzanine lounge of New York's Earl Carroll Theater, whose designer, Joseph J. Babolnay, collaborated with architect George Keister, was an elegant space, enlivened by figural statuary and touches of metal on plasterwork. Its walls and ceiling were painted olive green, its carpet was a darker green. Built in 1930-31, the theatre was later demolished.

On the East Coast, there were a wide variety of Art Deco cinemas by Eberson and others in Washington, D.C.; Philadelphia's State and Uptown theatres; several cinemas in Baltimore and elsewhere by Baltimorean John J. Zink; the Cape Cinema in Dennis, Massachusetts, the Cinema Theatre (ex-'French Casino') of Old Miami Beach, and countless more theatres up, down and inland from the Atlantic. But New York City – all five of its boroughs, not just Manhattan – boasted outstanding cinemas and, of course, legitimate theatres (though Los Angeles was undoubtedly the leader in Art Deco cinema designs). Among its jewels were Brooklyn's St. George Playhouse (with lounge furniture by Wolfgang Hoffmann), Staten Island's Paramount and Manhattan's Earl Carroll, Max Reinhardt and Ziegfeld theatres – and, of course, Donald Deskey's Radio City Music Hall complex (including the RKO Center Theater). The Earl Carroll Theater, whose designer, Joseph J. Babolnay, collaborated with architect George Keister, was an elegant, streamlined space – but not totally devoid of figural statuary and florid patterns, these on the carpets and upholstery. Built in 1930-31, the Earl Carroll was later, unfortunately, demolished. The same fate met Joseph Urban's old Ziegfeld Theater of c.1927, which was torn down around 1966.

The RKO Center Theater, which was considerably smaller than its Rockefeller Center neighbour, the Radio City Music Hall, opened to glowing reviews in 1933. Unlike its grand counterpart, however, the Center Theater, as it became known (there was also the nearby RKO Roxy theater, designed and built for S. L. Rothafel by Walter S. Ahlschlager in 1927, in the 'Portuguese Rococo' style), was a subtle, refined and unfortunately short-lived space, designed by Eugene Schoen (with the approval of Deskey, who was not able to juggle the designs of both theatres, as commissioned) and admired for its distinctive combination of beauty, comfort and a warm palette. Among its interior features was an illuminated glass mural by Maurice Heaton.

Donald Deskey's splendid interiors for the larger Radio City Music Hall still stand as a testament to the achievement of this vastly talented man. With a main auditorium seating 6,200 people (the Center accommodated 3,500 originally, Rothafel's former RKO Roxy 5,920) and a variety of ancillary public and private spaces, the Radio City Music Hall became the undisputed star of the entire Rockefeller Center complex. Donald Deskey received the commission to design the Music Hall's interiors in June 1932, after winning a competition sponsored by Todd & Brown, a firm representing the financial interests of the Rockefeller clan. Samuel Lionel 'Roxy' Rothafel, manager of the Music Hall project, originally wanted a cinema in the same 'Portuguese Rococo' style of the RKO Roxy, with which he had been associated formerly. Deskey managed to relieve Roxy of this concept and instead deliver what he called a 'Modern Rococo' design.

A review of the Art Deco interior would not be complete without looking at examples of that ultimate, essentially *faux*-interior, which was figuratively entered into by million of moviegoers the world over every week in the 1920s and 1930s: the Moderne movie set. In fact, wealthy clients sometimes commissioned interior designers to replicate a favourite set for their homes (some Hollywood art directors 'moonlighted' for private clients doing just this). Even major designers of domestic and other interiors lent a hand to creating film sets, among them Pierre Chareau, Michel Dufet, Paul Iribe, Robert Mallet-Stevens, Emile-Jacques Ruhlmann, Joseph Urban and Kem Weber.

Among the notable French films with Art Deco interiors were Marcel L'Herbier's *L'Inhumaine* (1923), whose exterior sets were by Mallet-Stevens and whose furnishings included designs by Chareau, Lalique, Puiforcat and Jean Luce; jewellery was provided by Raymond Templier, fashions by Paul Poiret and a futuristic laboratory set was concocted by painter Fernand Léger. Two young film-set designers, Claude Autant-Lara and Alberto Cavalcanti, provided additional sets, including a dramatic, mostly black-and-white dining room with Cubist, elongated diamond-back chairs and a raised floor section with an abstract, architectonic motif. Director L'Herbier's films made extensive use of Modernist interiors, others being *Le Carnaval des Vérités* (1920, with designs by Michel Dufet), *Le Vertige* (1926), *Villa Destin* (1921; designed in the style of Paul Poiret by Georges Lepape, one of the couturier's fashion illustrators) and *L'Argent* (1928), awash with indirect lighting, lacquer, leather and chrome. *Le P'tit Parigot* (1926), directed by René Le Somptier, featured sets by Robert and Sonia Delaunay, these a harmonious mélange of rectilinear and circular motifs (whose colours must have been bold and bright, though of course this did not matter too much in a black-and-white film). Jacques Feyder's *Les Nouveaux Messieurs* (1928), whose art director was Russian-born Lazare Meerson, was dramatically modern à la Le Corbusier, with an open plan, glass walls and modern European and tribal African art.

Hollywood sets, in all their satin splendour, gilded opulence and escapist glory, provided examples of the ultimate Art Deco interiors – and so often the only familiar ones – to millions of starstruck moviegoers: from the elaborate, showy backdrops used in Busby Berkeley's series of *Gold Diggers* spectaculars, to the variety of romantic nightclub dancefloors on which Fred twirled Ginger, from the chic urban, and urbane, penthouses and offices of *Five and Ten*, *Our Dancing Daughters*, *The Single Standard* and *Topper*, to the transoceanic and train travels depicted in *Dodsworth*, *Letty Lynton*, *Reaching for the Moon*, *Sweet Music* (with its streamlined locomotive), *Transatlantic*, *Twentieth Century*, and a film partly set on the *Normandie*, *Paris-New York* (the French-made *Les Perles de la Couronne* of 1937 was also shot aboard the luxury liner).

Indian films assumed Moderne looks, even fantasy pictures such as this one, *Amar Jyoti* ('Immortal Flame'), which told the story of a woman's revolt against male tyranny. The stylized, rather futuristic architectonic elements became all the more dramatic by virtue of their uniformly light palette.

Many of the finest Art Deco sets in Hollywood were created by art director Cedric Gibbons (1893-1960), a prolific, eclectic designer who worked for Samuel Goldwyn from 1918 to 1924, then for MGM from 1924 onwards. Designer also of the Art Deco-style 'Oscar' statuette in 1927, Gibbons visited the 1925 Paris Exposition, a not surprising revelation, considering the high-style Art Deco sheen given to many of his sets. One of his finest films was *Our Dancing Daughters* (1928), considered by Howard Mandelbaum and Eric Myers, co-authors of the superb paean to 1920s and 1930s Hollywood design, *Screen Deco*, 'the first American movie to fully exploit the new Modernist decor'. And exploit it did, with a Ruhlmannesque divan topped with tasselled pillows and fronting a silver-leafed and lacquered stepped screen. His 1929 film, *Dynamite*, included a copy of *Les Perruches*, a painting by Jean Dupas which had featured in Ruhlmann's pavilion at the 1925 Paris fair.

After Gibbons, probably the best-known art director-designer working in the Art Deco style was Van Nest Polglase, head of RKO's art department in the 1930s. Polglase's *The Magnificent Flirt* (1928), according to its public-relations people, made extensive use of 'the new French Decorative Art'. One of its sets, a bathroom, featured a sunken marble tub with a gilded stylized-mask spout. A wide stepped-pyramid of shelving, a relief snail shell on its sides, was laden with perfume bottles and stood between the bath and a streamlined dressing table with a huge circular mirror; both table and tub were set under niches of concave scallop shells. Polglase also worked on *Top Hat* and numerous other Fred Astaire-Ginger Rogers films (and he and his RKO colleagues even designed Ginger's own house).

Joseph Urban's contributions to film design may not be as well known as his hotels, casinos, nightclubs and theatres, but they were fairly extensive, including some thirty films he designed while head of William Randolph Hearst's Cosmopolitan Productions in the 1920s.

IN PARIS AS WELL as London, New York as well as Los Angeles, and elsewhere throughout Europe and North America, retail firms – cosmetics companies, fashion houses, department stores among them – were having shops, offices, showrooms and elaborate window displays created for them in the Art Deco style. Even small, independent businesses – beauty salons, barber shops, shoe stores, dry cleaners – jumped on the Modernist bandwagon. Parisian designers such as Ruhlmann, Rateau, Süe et Mare, Mallet-Stevens and Lalique received commissions from major retailers, couturiers, perfumers and the like (including some from foreign clients) and in America Donald Deskey, Ely Jacques Kahn and Russel Wright were among the notables responsible for creating such interiors.

René Lalique not only designed the interiors of his own showrooms, but he also created interior designs for a variety of clients, among them John Wanamaker's Philadelphia men's store, for which he provided huge etched-glass panels of monumental Neoclassical figures; the *parfumeurs* Roger et Gallet and Worth (for which he also produced scent bottles); the New York retailer Jay Thorpe, and the Los Angeles retailer Alexander & Oviatt, whose president, James Oviatt, commissioned moulded-glass lift doors, mail boxes and other metalwork, and an illuminated glass ceiling from Lalique (the Paris firm Saddier et Fils also worked on the decoration). Most of Lalique's interiors, not surprisingly, incorporated much of his own uncoloured glass, but others were more colourful and exotic, less glass-oriented. A *c.*1925 Paris showroom for Roger et Gallet, for instance, was totally decked out – from the carpeted floors to the walls and vaulted ceiling – with a pattern of showy birds of paradise and tropical plants in shades of black, gold and green; this was in fact a large-scale version of the design for the packaging of the Roget et Gallet scent, *Le Jade*.

Lalique also designed a showroom for couturière Madeleine Vionnet in 1923, in collaboration with Georges de Feure and Chanut, the architect of the Galeries Lafayette. Three handsome arches, with armatures of nickelled metal and containing flower-bedecked panels of pressed glass, dominated the grand salon, and overhead was a rose window of glass. Horizontal panels with floral and foliage designs ranged around the room at the tops of the walls, with vertical panels painted with stylishly clad women (these by de Feure). The overall, harmonious effect of this light-coloured room, which also contained furniture of a light wood, was elegant and spectacular, and the salon proved a fine example of decorative architectural glass in a large space.

Just as numerous New York retail stores had ridden the Art Deco wave in terms of promoting both European and domestic contemporary designs, so several of them duly refurbished their interiors or at the least contained showrooms designed in the Moderne taste. The new store built by the retailer Stewart & Co. around 1930, for instance, included, among other elements, lovely vertical plasterwork panels throughout, designed by sculptor Jacques Carlu and comprising rows of single large triangles surmounted by bas-reliefs of modish women and canines. Ely Jacques Kahn's showroom for Yardley & Co. was simple and Modernist, with fluted metal and wood details on the furniture and mouldings and comfortable, leather-covered armchairs. Interestingly, Ruhlmann furnished Yardley's London showroom in the early 1930s, with a handsome rectilinear display desk, cupboard and chairs, these largely of Macassar ebony (in 1924 he had provided furniture for Yardley's Paris branch).

In Chicago Philip B. Maher designed a lovely French-inspired showroom for Stanley Korshak's Blackstone Shop, a women's clothing store. Elegant contemporary furniture, of grey wood with green-satin upholstery, paid homage to eighteenth-century French design, specifically the Directoire style. In Los Angeles there was Bullock's Wilshire Department Store (John and Donald Parkinson, 1928), whose decorative tour-de-force was Herman Sachs's 1929 ceiling fresco, *Speed of Transportation*, in the motor court, a vividly hued visual paean to travel and transport, including such images as a winged-footed and -hatted Mercury, the Graf Zeppelin, an ocean liner, locomotive and quartet of silver-grey aeroplanes. The fresco was just one of many examples of Modernist decoration inside the elegant store, whose co-founder, P. G. Winnett, had visited the 1925 Paris Exposition and was eager to have Bullock's interior and exterior reflect the contemporary design style.

In London assorted shops and stores were decorated partly or wholly in the Moderne vein. Even the venerable Harrods succumbed, featuring a Streamline Moderne barber shop and hairdressing salon and elegant Modernist boardroom in the 1930s. Austin Reed's men's shop in Regent Street, designed by P. J. Westwood, boasted arguably the most up-to-date 'tonsorial parlour' in Britain.

DOZENS OF HOTELS in large cities throughout the world were designed wholly or partly in the Art Deco style, their public rooms – restaurants, bars, lobbies – as well as private accommodations containing largely mass-produced furnishings, but in numerous cases enhanced by custom-designed hand-made interior details, foremost among these decorative wrought-iron work (balustrades, fireplace grilles, doors), painted and/or bas-relief sculpted murals or panels, and patterned carpets.

Four of London's major hotels, the Strand Palace, the Park Lane, Claridge's and the Savoy, were built or redesigned in the late 1920s and 1930s and included outstanding Art Deco features in their lavish interiors. Elsewhere in Great Britain, several hotels were built in the late 1920s and 1930s, mostly in coastal resort areas, which struck Art Deco themes both inside and out. For instance, Burgh Island in Bigbury-on-Sea, off the coast of South Devon, was designed by architect Matthew Dawson and constructed in 1929.

Hotels with Art Deco interior elements featured in other European, North African and Middle Eastern cities as well, although not as many in Paris as one might expect. The Hotel George V, whose architects were G. Lefranc and G. Kybo, was built in 1926 and contained several elegant Art Deco rooms, and the Ritz redesigned one of its dining rooms in the 1930s, its salient feature a stylized fantastic hunting scene (there is also Art Deco-era ornamental wrought-iron on some of its staircases).

The Moroccan city of Marrakesh, with its rich French-laced Arabic culture, was the site of a splendid Art Deco-era hotel, La Mamounia. Named after a verdant desert oasis, the sumptuous hotel contained numerous hybrid-exotic interiors which boast a great many Gallic-influenced furnishings.

In Hamburg there was the Hotel Vier Jahreszeiten, with its *c.*1920 bar, as well as the reception room of the Hotel Duisburger. Amsterdam's American Hotel, like many other Continental hotels of the time, was aglow with ceilings and light fixtures with strong Art Deco overtones. In the Far East, Shanghai was a popular spot with well-to-do European tourists in the 1920s and 1930s, hence many of its hotels built in those decades incorporated Art Deco elements in their interior design. Australia, too, was the site of Art Deco hotels, among them the Pier Hotel in Manly, New South Wales, designed by Emil Sodersten and including much Monel metal (a nickel-silver alloy produced by the German-based Mond Nickel Company) and black glass in its public rooms.

Most of North America's larger cities seemed to boast an Art Deco hotel, or at least an earlier hotel with several rooms furnished in that style, usually a dining or reception area. There were New York's Waldorf-Astoria and St. George Hotel, the latter in Brooklyn and designed in part by Winold Reiss; Phoenix's Aztec-inspired Arizona Biltmore, whose consulting architect was Frank Lloyd Wright; the Mayfair in Los Angeles, with a gleaming Streamline Moderne ballroom by Kem Weber; Toronto's Royal York; the Carlton and the Shoreham in Washington, D.C.; and the superb Starrett Netherland Plaza in Cincinnati, which was recently refurbished by Rita St. Clair, who kept its outstanding murals, metalwork and other architectural details intact. Some of America's most joyful and colourful hotels (and apartment buildings) arose in Miami Beach in the 1930s, and although their pastel-painted, nautical- and tropical-motif-strewn façades are familiar to many, their interiors are less celebrated, largely because they have not fared as well as the exteriors in terms of preservation (in some cases they have been destroyed altogether, such as the lovely Hotel Helene, whose lounge featured brightly coloured geometric-patterned carpets, Modernist metal standard lamps and ash-stands, and over-stuffed armchairs of the tub and square varieties).

In Britain, the spectrum of places to eat out, or have a drink or two, was wide and varied, and included notable examples in the Modernist style. Oliver P. Bernard, who designed the interiors of several London hotels, was also responsible for a new type of public interior in London in the 1930s, the Corner Houses and snack bars managed by J. Lyons & Co. (these also were built in Liverpool and other urban areas). Surfaces gleamed from the use of copper and aluminium tiles, handsome ornamental patterns covered walls and comprised entryways, railings and light fixtures, and the overall ambience of most of these Lyons facilities was airy, comfortable and welcoming. One Corner House included a huge octagonal counter in the middle surrounded by a bevy

The bar in Hamburg's Hotel Vier Jahreszeiten, *c.* 1920, featured wall panels with an Oriental theme (on the right), as well as an elegant Moderne balustrade with a trim geometric design.

of round stools by P.E.L., giant stone pillars topped by stylized lotus blossoms of light, a floor covered with a bold geometric design, and a good many tables and chairs for more private dining.

Somewhat akin to Bernard's Corner Houses and cafés were the many stainless-steel- and other metal-clad diners that began to be built in the United States in the 1920s (peaking in the 1940s). Glistening chromed interiors featured long counters fronted by a line of stools, with private booths next to the front windows. Floors were often covered with bright geometric patterns, glass bricks comprised some of the walls and assorted Art Deco motifs, most predominantly the sunray, could be found on the metal-clad walls. Most of these popular cafés were created anonymously, but well-known designers sometimes lent their hands to such projects, such as Donald Deskey's café-cum-soda fountain (c. 1929-30) for the Abraham and Straus department store in Brooklyn. The handsome tubular-steel chairs and backed stools were produced by Ypsilanti Reed Furniture, and fluorescent lighting, mirrored walls and assorted horizontal elements featured.

In Australia there were the milk bars, a local invention which spread to England (the first ever was The Milky Way in Melbourne, designed by Roy Grounds). These were thoroughly modern, even futuristic-looking glass- and metal-clad establishments that came complete with tubular-steel chairs, smartly curving counters and stylized 1930s-style lettering on their welcoming neon signs. Drinks other than milk were imbibed in Australia, of course, and one of the country's smartest cocktail bars in the Art Deco style could be found at the Paragon Restaurant in Katoomba, New South Wales.

In North America, besides the many walk-in and drive-up snack bars that proliferated in the 1930s (cars were becoming a way of life, and diners and other eating establishments were built to accommodate plenty of parked vehicles), there were of course bigger, largely more elegant urban bars and restaurants that generally catered to a more sophisticated, exclusive clientele. In New York, *émigré* designer Winold Reiss created one of the most exuberant dining rooms for the Alamac Hotel: the African-theme Congo Room of 1923. In the roof garden dining room of Manhattan's St. Regis Hotel, another European-born designer, Joseph Urban, created an exotic, flamboyant eating space dominated by a lush floor-to-ceiling painting of long-tailed tropical birds in blossom-bedecked trees. Without a theme, but a striking urban dining space nonetheless, was the Manhattan Room of the Hotel New Yorker, a largely wood-panelled and red-leather-covered room with an array of geometric patterns, notably on the tablecloths. In Chicago the 'Moderne Room' of the Lauer Sisters' Restaurant (c. 1936) was a sleek, brightly coloured dining area, with yellow-and-blue covered tubular-metal armchairs, tables with the same colour scheme and equally vivid hues on the walls, which also featured

The marble- and walnut-sheathed lobby of the Kennedy Warren apartment hotel (1932) in Washington, D.C., was an airy, elegant space. A mélange of Neoclassical and Moderne elements, its high, beamed ceiling was painted with rising suns, zigzags, Greek crosses and other motifs.

bas-relief roundels of Neoclassical figures and giant silhouettes of stylized plant forms.

THE INTERIORS OF Manhattan's ever-rising skyscrapers led the world in terms of sheer exuberance and imagination vis-à-vis commercial structures, their ground-floor lobbies and other public (and even private) spaces especially subjected to a wealth of stylized geometric motifs, innovative and sometimes opulent materials, and often outstanding examples of period sculptures and paintings. Likewise, civic buildings – such as post offices, city halls, assorted regional governmental headquarters, even war memorials – proved impressive monumental structures, their interiors often grand-scale spaces including many of the same sculpted stone and ornamental metalwork details as their expressive exteriors.

Among the most significant commercial interiors in New York City were those of the Chrysler and Chanin buildings, Rockefeller Center and the smaller, lesser-known Film Center of Ely Jacques Kahn, but nearly as exciting were dozens of newly executed banks and office buildings in the Wall Street and Midtown areas and elsewhere – their metal mail chutes and boxes embellished with stylized reliefs, their entrance and lift doors agleam with conventionalized flora and fauna, their marble and terrazzo floors and walls chock-a-block with Moderne forms and geometric patterns.

The massive Rockefeller Center (Hood & Fouilhoux; Reinhard & Hofmeister; Corbett, Harrison & MacMurray, 1931-40) was both an architectural masterwork and an artistic triumph. The jewel of the whole complex was Radio City Music Hall, whose interior design was in part created and totally coordinated by Donald Deskey. The array of gifted artists, sculptors, metalworkers and other artisans whose talents were gathered together to embellish the huge public spaces of the Center with murals, reliefs and three-dimensional sculptures made up a list of America's leading artistic lights: sculptors Paul Manship, Isamu Noguchi, Lee Lawrie, Leo Friedlander, Gaston Lachaise and William Zorach; painters José María Sert, Diego Rivera (whose controversial mural, containing the images of Lenin and other Communists, was eventually rejected by Nelson Rockefeller) and Yosuo Kuniyoshi; ceramicist Henry Varnum Poor, textile designer Ruth Reeves, and even photographers Margaret Bourke-White and Edward Steichen.

Other towering, stepped civic or commercial structures – or more horizontally massive piles – throughout America's major urban areas contained interiors whose elaborate metal-enhanced, painted, lacquered, mosaic-covered, marble-sheathed and chandelier-hung public spaces qualify them as outstanding Art Deco edifices. Among these commercial or civic 'palaces' were the Richfield Oil Company building, Los Angeles; the Gulf Building, Houston;

the Nebraska State Capitol in Lincoln; the American National Bank Building, Chicago; the Union Trust Company and Fisher Buildings, Detroit; the Circle Tower Building, Indianapolis; City Hall in Kalamazoo, Michigan; Northwestern Bell Telephone, Minneapolis; the Milwaukee Gas Light Company, and the Kansas City Power and Light Co. Building. Geometric and architectonic design elements abounded in just about all of these buildings, as did stylized human, plant, animal and bird forms (the American eagle took on myriad guises on ubiquitous mail boxes). The San Francisco Stock Exchange featured a Diego Rivera mural representing work and workers, and the city's Medical and Dental Building boasted an interior rife with Meso-American motifs.

The S.C. Johnson Administration Building in Racine, Wisconsin, designed and furnished by Frank Lloyd Wright in the late 1930s, was probably *the* outstanding harmonious Modernist workplace in the United States. A massive streamlined brick and glass structure, the building features an assortment of curves, ovals and circles in its interior, from a circle-embellished ceiling in the reception area, to tubes of translucent Pyrex used as wall partitions and skylights throughout, to the huge workroom, its high ceiling seemingly supported by a mass of piers shaped like giant golf tees.

Although the most exciting developments in the design of the interiors of large buildings were undoubtedly happening in the United States in the late 1920s and 1930s, some outstanding European structures boasted harmonious public spaces of world renown. One of the most splendid is the Reception Hall of London's Daily Express Building (1929-32) in Fleet Street, designed by Robert Atkinson and admired by John Betjeman for its 'wonderful rippling confections of metal'. Allegorical panels – huge figures depicting the 'Six Ages of Architecture' – featured on the new headquarters of the Royal Institute of British Architects (1931-34) in Portland Place, London, these in the form of six glass door panels, acid-engraved and then sand-blasted to the design of Raymond McGrath.

Other municipal and commercial buildings throughout Europe displayed Art Deco elements, although none with the eclectic verve of North American interiors. In Paris, for instance, Emile-Jacques Ruhlmann designed interiors for the New York City Bank around 1930, basically small spaces with austere, rectilinear and private settings. A grand interior space *was* created by Ruhlmann, however, this the ballroom (Salle des Fêtes) of the Chambre de Commerce of 1927, with its massive ribbed pilasters and two rows of six large wedding-cake-like chandeliers, consisting of pendent rows of crystal beads (like those in the 1925 Hôtel du Collectionneur); matching lights clung to the walls, strip lights were concealed in the cornice and the ribbed motif was repeated on other surfaces as well.

The cast-aluminium, eagle-adorned light fixture perched at the bottom of a stairway in City Hall, Kalamazoo, Michigan, is a defiantly modern architectonic element amid a jungle of Neoclassical scrolls and tendrils.

In France, the birthplace of Art Deco, few public edifices were custom-built and -designed in the 1920s-30s style; instead, most such interiors were refurbishments of earlier structures (as with Ruhlmann's Chambre de Commerce). Two outstanding contemporary designs could be found in municipal buildings, however: Gustave Louis Jaulmes's c. 1935 Town Hall of the Fifth Arrondissement of Paris, and Rheims City Hall, whose architects were Bouchette and Expert, but whose tour-de-force design was provided by metalworker Raymond Subes.

The Anzac Memorial of 1934, built in Sydney's Hyde Park to commemorate the dead of World War I, is arguably one of the handsomest public structures in the world designed in the Art Deco period. The red granite edifice, by C. Bruce Dellit (1900-1942), features an amber window on every side, each with a design of the Anzac rising sun (the same motif appears on the badge of the Australian Military forces, so it is not simply intended here as a typical Art Deco period device).

THERE WERE CHAPELS and churches in the 1920s whose altars, pulpits, seating, metalwork, stained-glass windows, even statuary and Stations of the Cross (among the latter were Eric Gill's bas-reliefs for London's Westminster Cathedral) were very much in the Art Deco style (synagogues, too, contained the occasional Art Deco reference). In France, the windows, ceiling, altar screens and other elements in the soaring, vaulted, neo-Gothic interior of Auguste Perret's 1922-23 church at Raincy featured crosses, circles and diamonds with either a vertical or horizontal line across them. In St. Helier, on the island of Jersey, the ubiquitous René Lalique designed, along with British architect A. B. Grayson, a new interior for the church of St. Matthew, which was on the property of Florence, Lady Trent, widow of Jesse Boot (of the chemist Boots). Lalique had already designed at least one altar before the one in Jersey, the 1930 Chapelle de la Vierge Fidèle in Caen. The Frenchman's 1934 contributions to the refurbishment of the Victorian house of worship comprised a new high altar with illuminated cross behind, aside of which were two floriate glass columns; side walls of glass panels surrounding the vestry and a smaller chapel with altar; a water font; the altar rail; windows, and other details, even the door handles. A lovely refuge of crystalline splendour and purity, St. Matthew's is dominated by the massive frosted-glass cross and two flanking pillars, all of which are decorated at the top with moulded blossoms of the Regal lily (*Lilium regale*), better known as the 'Jersey lily', which also appears on the four stainless-steel-framed screen walls and windows (they appear as buds, not blossoms, on the latter). The smaller Lady Chapel has a reredos comprising tall relief panels of angels, their hands clasped and heads bowed in prayer, and the altar rail is adorned with the Madonna lily (*Lilium candidium*).

In Britain, several Modern Movement architect-designers created houses of worship in the 1930s. Francis X. Velarde's St. Gabriel, Blackburn, dating from 1933, made a strong contemporary statement. The red-brick interior of St. Saviour in Eltham (Welch, Cachemaille-Day & Lander, 1932-33) was not as idiosyncratic, but its unusual flat roof (St. Gabriel had a traditional high vaulted ceiling), tall thin blue-glass windows and architectonic concrete reredos, with a massive Modernistic Christ figure at the centre, were far from the ecclesiastical norm.

Not only did Manhattan's skyscrapers contain handsome Art Deco interiors, but so, surprisingly, did a handful of its newly built ecclesiastical buildings, as well as others in the United States. The chancel of the Church of the Heavenly Rest (*c.* 1929-30), for instance, featured a soaring architectonic stone reredos that could have exactly replicated the silhouette of a stepped office tower, had it not been for the cross in the middle and the pair of kneeling, praying angels atop the pinnacles at either side.

Church exteriors did not often assume Modernist appearances, but those of schools – from elementary level to advanced colleges of art – were often bedecked with Art Deco motifs, lettering and reliefs. Less so their interiors, although there were some outstanding exceptions. One, in Michigan, was Eliel Saarinen's Kingswood School for Girls, at Cranbrook in Bloomfield Hills. The 1929-31 school, along with the other educational and residential components of the Cranbrook Academy of Art complex of which Saarinen became head in 1932, was a joint family effort: Saarinen's wife, Loja, designed its curtains and carpets, and his son, Eero, created furniture for it.

The urban-sophisticated sets of *The Kiss* (*bottom*), a 1929 silent film (MGM's last) starring Greta Garbo (here talking to a stern Anders Randolf), were the work of Cedric Gibbons, arguably Hollywood's top art director-designer working in the Art Deco style. The strong geometric elements here – the base of the table, the fireplace and the artwork over it – owe a debt to Cubism, while the covering on the sofa has Native American overtones.

Production designer William Cameron Menzies created a sleek, horizontally striated environment for the bedroom of Douglas Fairbanks, Sr. (here with Edward Everett Horton), in the 1931 film *Reaching for the Moon* (*below*). The low semicircular-arched screen, curving end tables attached to the bed and conical-shaded lamps added further Moderne fillips.

In *Women Love Diamonds* (*top*), American silent-screen star Pauline Starke wore an overflowing dressing gown whose dizzying pattern was more than a match for the hotch-potch of Moderne, rococo and kitsch elements and motifs crowding her bedroom-boudoir. The film dates from 1927.

British films, too, featured Modernist sets, like the smart curved and stepped bedroom (*above*) from *Captivation* (1931). The actress is Betty Stockfield, who stands on a bold Moderne rug (another example is on the floor on the left; yet another is thrown on the bed behind).

The combined talents of director Cecil B. de Mille and art director Cedric Gibbons gave the 1929 film *Dynamite* as much of an impact as its title. In the words of one critic, it was 'exuberant, wonderfully vigorous' and a film which 'skilfully evokes the look and character of the Jazz Age'. Note the reproduction of Jean Dupas's *Les Perruches* (see page 36) at the top of the marble staircase, where Kay Johnson gives a sidelong glance to Charles Bickford.

Britain's trains in the 1920s and 1930 tended to the tubular-steel Modernist rather than decorative plush style, although the 1937 LNER *Coronation* featured overstuffed seats with handsome chevron upholstery in the First Class car (*right*). Elaborate light fixtures and shiny florid mouldings also decorated that coach and the equally plush observation car (*below*). (Note the thistles and the rose on the overdoor decoration leading to the curved-ceiling observation car.)

The Orient Express, of all European trains, evokes the most mystery, romance and period flavour. Production designer Tony Walton added a touch of glass – and homage to Lalique – to his sets for the 1974 film *Murder on the Orient Express*. In this scene (*above*), a seated Albert Finney, as Hercule Poirot, speaks to Sean Connery. In fact, Lalique's original moulded and acid-decorated glass and wood partitions were designed for numerous Wagons-Lits cars, including the opulent *Côte d'Azur*, from which this example (*left*) comes.

Several American rail terminals were outstanding examples of Art Deco both inside and out. Foremost among them was the Cincinnati Union Terminal (Fellheimer & Wagner, 1929-33). A massive stepped stone structure, its domed interior (*above*) featured Winold Reiss's glass-mosaic mural and additional panels depicting the history of transportation. For its ladies' lounge (*opposite left*), Jean Bourdelle provided linoleum wall panels carved with a peacock, panther, monkeys and other creatures occupying an earth-toned jungle. Paul Philippe Cret, a University of Pennsylvania professor, was the 'aesthetic advisor' responsible for transforming the station's original Neoclassical plans into a contemporary Moderne scheme.

Airports, built in profusion in the 1930s, often contained public areas with handsome Modernist touches. The waiting room of Oklahoma's Tulsa Municipal Airport Administration Building (*above right*), designed by Frederick Vance Kershner in 1932, was one such space, with smart Art Deco lighting fixtures and other period details enlivening what could so easily have been a dull, cavernous expanse.

Top industrial designers in the United States, like Raymond Loewy, Gilbert Rohde and Norman Bel Geddes, lent their talents to designing Modernist train interiors. This bar car (*right*) is a dark-toned, masculine space, the two russet-coloured lighting panels overhead curving at the end to act as vertical dividers for the built-in bar's shelves.

The public rooms of the *Normandie*, which was launched in May 1935, glistened with mirrored and plain glass, gold and silver leaf, and masses of artificial light. The First Class dining room, seen on this page, was a latter-day Galerie des Glaces. At the entrance were gilt-stucco wall panels (*left*), one by Raymond Delamarre depicting *Les Arts et les Monuments Normands*, the other *Les Sports et les Jeux* by Léon Drivier. Other reliefs were at the far end of the 305-foot long room (*above*), where *La Paix*, a gilt-bronze figure by Louis Dejean, stood watch. In between 200 tables and over twice as many chairs were set amid a shimmering, windowless (but air-conditioned) hall illuminated by René Lalique. Massive pendent ceiling *lustres* were at either end; the walls were veneered in hammered-glass panels interspersed with over thirty elongated lighting fixtures, and twelve fountains of light on pedestals added to the sparkling atmosphere.

The *Normandie*'s Grand Salon (*above*) was dominated by a four-part allegorical mural created by Jean Dupas. Its subject was the history of the sea and navigation, and it was related within contexts both mythological (such as the chariot of Poseidon and the birth of Aphrodite) and quasi-historical (depictions of galleons, steamships etc.). The 30-foot-high masterwork was executed in the *verre églomisé* technique, whereby panels of plate glass were painted on the reverse, then embellished with gold and silver leaf, and finally affixed to canvas backing. Aubusson-tapestry-covered chairs and sofas, rosy red and abloom with floral designs, were scattered about the room, and artificial light emanated from five-tiered 'fountains' centring circular banquettes. Two banquettes surrounded huge decorative pewter urns by Maurice Daurat.

The Grand Salon led to the Smoking Room (*right*), largely the work of Jean Dunand. Four lacquered bas-relief panels dominated this massive, masculine space; they depicted the leisure-time pursuits of fishing and other sports on one side, grape harvesting and taming horses on the other (the two seen here). The furniture was simple, solid, dark-lacquered and comfortable.

LE GRAND SALON CARRÉ DES PREMIÈRES CLASSES

The *Atlantique* was another French ship known for its splendid modern décor, much of it orchestrated in lacquer by Jean Dunand. Owned by the Compagnie Sud-Atlantique, the vessel made its first voyage to Buenos Aires in 1931 (unfortunately, it was destroyed by fire in 1933). In the elegant First Class Grand Salon (*opposite below*) were soaring walls of green and pink marble, and a sculpture by Raymond Rivoire (*bottom right*) depicted a twentieth-century Diana walking a greyhound.

The French Line's opulent Art Deco fleet also included the *Ile-de-France*, launched in 1926. Coming hot on the heels of the Paris Exposition, the *Ile* proved a worthy ambassadress for her country and a fitting vehicle for the *années folles* that held the affluent world in thrall. Ruhlmann designed its elegant tearoom (*opposite below*), with wall panels, chairs, tables and piano of white ash. Massive Sèvres *vases réflecteurs* occupied pedestals, and on the wall was a lush panel by Jean Dupas depicting various idle-rich amusements. The *Ile*'s First Class dining room (*opposite right*) featured grey marble walls, 112 illuminated squares of moulded Lalique glass and an architectonic fountain by Henri Navarre. The room's overall design was by Pierre Patout (architect of Ruhlmann's Hôtel du Collectionneur at the 1925 fair), and the massive oval hunting scene was the work of Eddy Legrand and Léon Voguet.

The Cunard-White Star liner, the *Queen Mary*, was launched in 1936. The monumental vessel was meant to rival the *Normandie* and was not without wonderful Modernist touches – although a few seemed to be lifted outright from the French *paquebots*, such as the massive metal-banded vases-on-pedestals in its Cabin Class lounge. The smart wood-veneered and chromed-metal cocktail bar (*above right*) was encircled by red-leather stools and enlivened overhead by A. R. Thomson's mural of a festive scene honouring the Silver Jubilee of George V. The blue- and cream-coloured Cabin Class swimming pool (*right*), highlighted with bands of green and red and a panel of exotic birds behind the diving board, was a capacious, almost theatrical space.

S. Charles Lee orchestrated the interior of Los Angeles's Wiltern Theater in 1929-31 (now restored) (*above*) wherein the audience is enveloped and bedazzled by a veritable galaxy of Art Deco. Gold-painted stars on the ceiling encircle a massive sunburst, which emits gilded rays comprising scrolls, chevrons, smaller rays and geometric devices. The asbestos fire curtain is covered with a silvery and pastel fairyland landscape-cum-cityscape, complete with golden skyscrapers and a rippling waterfall.

In 1937 John Eberson, the Austrian-born, New York-based architect, designed the Colony Theater (*left*) in Cleveland, Ohio, its elegantly streamlined interior distinguished by the broad, dramatic sweeps of soothing colours. Eberson also designed cinemas in Washington, D.C., and was the co-creator of the Rex in Paris in 1932.

In Aurora, Illinois, the interior of the restored 1931 Paramount cinema (*opposite*) exudes Italian-Renaissance-gone-Moderne splendour. Painted views of Venice are overhung with trees bearing Art Deco flowerbursts and bells, and stylized volutes, wings and sunrays vie with classical anthemions and palmettes, making for a colourful, evocative, albeit distracting, fantasy environment.

The well-maintained Muswell Hill Odeon (*below*) features a smart interior of the graduated-pastel-hued, Streamline Moderne variety. Its lighting fixtures are especially attractive, notably the illuminated ribbon running down the middle of the ceiling to the top of the screen, and the circular light nestled in the recessed ceiling area (*left*).

The peach-coloured panel in the centre of this photograph of the Liverpool Forum (*right*) (now a Cannon cinema) is decorated in relief with two fanciful Manhattan-style skyscrapers linked by a stone bridge over a winding river. The stylized fountain motif dominating the private box to the left is a variation on a theme prevalent in the Art Deco repertoire. The apricot-peach-salmon palette is a soothing one often found in restored 1930s cinemas (though it is not always authentic).

Among Britain's premier Art Deco cinemas were the unique, custom-built movie houses in the big cities. London's New Victoria Cinema, whose principal designer was E. Wamsley Lewis, was one of these. Inside the 1929-30 rectangular structure was an array of design elements with an underwater theme. In the auditorium (*left*) were shell-capped side lights, a fire curtain painted with mermaids and other marine life, and a carpet with a stylized wave pattern, while in the lobby areas (*above*) bas-reliefs of dolphins adorned the ceiling, saucy mermaids the metal railings and pairs of facing fish the scallop-shell overdoor lights. The predominant colour of this submarine fairyland was an appropriate blue-green (not the red seen in the *c.* 1980 photographs of what is now the Apollo Victoria legitimate theatre).

The back entrance of London's Savoy Theatre (*left*), decorated in 1929 by Basil Ionides (also in charge or refitting the Savoy Hotel), features a décor that is smartly Moderne, from the black marble pedestal surmounted by an exotic sculptural group in a fluted niche, to the stepped, undulating ceiling, with discreet lighting concealed at the top. The green paint was a recent addition and the walls and ceiling were originally in shades of cream and white; the interior of the theatre was gutted by fire in February 1990.

A little-known Art Deco treasure is Paris's gilded and blue Théâtre Daunou (*below left*), designed in 1921 by Armand-Albert Rateau (in collaboration with its owner Jeanne Lanvin and Paul Plumet). The seats, curtain and lapis-lazuli pilasters were the rich blue of cornflowers – sometimes called 'Bleu Lanvin' because it was so closely linked with the couturière – and gilt flora and fauna of Oriental inspiration occupied wall panels and the underside of the balcony. The most profuse blossom was the stylized marguerite.

European theatres and cinemas in both ornate Moderne and more minimalist Modernist guises were built in the 1920s and 1930s. One of the most elaborate was Amsterdam's Tuschinski theatre (today a Cannon cinema), created and furnished in 1918-21 by various members of the Amsterdam School as a flamboyant but nonetheless harmonious mixture of architectural and design components. From the colourful painted ceiling and carpeted floor in the lobby (*above*) by J. Gidding, to its elaborate light fittings (*opposite*), the Tuschinski remains a visionary, expressionistic 1920s setting.

Even London's venerable Harrods joined the *art moderne* crowd, in the 1930s designing its hairdressing salon (*left*) in a quasi-streamline manner, with smartly curved occasional tables and counters, boxy veneered chairs and an unusual fretwork ceiling border.

The barber shop in the Austin Reed store in London's Regent Street (*below*) dates from 1929-30 and was created by P. J. Westwood. It was arguably the most up-to-date 'tonsorial parlour' in Britain – a gleaming ovoid space of mirrors, Vitrolite, chrome, marble, frosted glass and, suspended from on high, continuous arcs of neon tubing forming an undulating wave.

Betty Joel created retail showrooms for herself and clients, as well as fulfilling a host of domestic commissions (including one from the Duchess of York, later Queen Elizabeth). The elegant, somewhat spare showroom (*right*) was designed in 1930 for the milliner Mary Manners in London's Bruton Street. Decoration is limited to the geometric patterns of upholstery, the sweeping abstracts of the area rugs and the simple fretwork of the ceiling light.

Small retail establishments also assumed chic Moderne looks, like this beauty parlour (*above*) in the Jefferson Hotel, St Louis, Missouri. Note especially the jazzily patterned upholstery and the profusion of unusual angles, such as the silhouettes of the doorways.

This high-ceilinged office area (*left*) was designed in the 1930s by John Duncan Miller, probably for a showroom. Except for the square armchair, the space is an essay in curvilinearity: in the abstract carpet, in the bird-and-wave motif curtains and in the lamp.

These two Modernist Chicago bars present variations on a metal-furniture theme. The Boulevard Bridge Restaurant's main floor bar (1933) (*below*) of walnut, lace wood and stainless steel is surrounded by no-nonsense metal stools. The four-part mural is by Hanns Teichert, who also provided the air-brush-effect visual double entendre on the wall of Harry's New York Bar (*c.* 1935) (*right*). The rather elegant metal-framed furniture was designed by Harry Lund and manufactured by Warren McArthur.

The wealthy patronized casinos, while the masses in the 1920s and 1930s escaped to the darkness of a cinema for entertainment. Frank Jay Gould's 'Palais de la Méditerranée' was a $5-million, 2-acre playground for the rich in Nice. Its bronze and marble stairway (*below*), surrounded by handsome wall lights and modish murals, was part of the 'unusual modernistic design' of this 'new rival of Monte Carlo' (according to a press release). Colourful geometric and abstract-modern motifs covered the carpet, wall and seat coverings in the casino's Baccarat Room (*left*), with a rather incongruous Venetian scene hanging over a sedate desk (actually 'the Bank', the $40-million Gould fortune the high rollers hoped to break).

The restaurant in New York's Central Park Casino (*above*) was designed by Joseph Urban *c.* 1929-30. It was a vibrant space awash with colourful stylized vegetation, from its frond-and-berry wallpaper (and similar floor covering), to the relief grape clusters winding their way around slim columns. Eddy Duchin and his orchestra entertained at the casino, which was deemed one of New York's 'newest and most beautiful' night spots.

ART DECO IN PUBLIC PLACES

Stylish Art Deco eating and drinking establishments dotted Europe, North America, even Australia. One of the smartest cocktail bars there was designed in 1931 by Henry White for the Paragon Restaurant in Katoomba, New South Wales (*below.*)

A striking urban dining and drinking place was the mid-1930s Manhattan Room of the Hotel New Yorker (*bottom*).

Paris's Vaudeville Brasserie (*opposite*) in the rue Vivienne is a glittering, marble-sheathed eating establishment that strongly evokes the elegance of the 1920s, when it first opened. With its Modernist lighting fixtures, exuberant bronze relief panels and sleek sculptures of Neoclassical-Moderne maidens, Le Vaudeville is an authentic Art Deco interior whose period splendour continues to shine, well over fifty years on.

A thoroughly Moderne cocktail bar (*above*) enlivened the older Carlton Hotel in Washington, D.C.. Boldly striped seating, crisp, round tables and mirrors, and a roundel with a Bacchic subject set the scene, but the *pièce de résistance* was the curvaceous bar, sheathed all round with glass panels etched with grapes and neoclassical figures. The bar's crowning glory was the three-dimensional goddess (*above right*), who could be made to float upwards and appear at the bar's summit.

In 1923, *émigré* designer **Winold Reiss** contributed wall-paintings and other decorations to one of New York's most exuberant, unusual restaurants, the Alamac Hotel's Congo Room (*right*). Jungle-scene murals, furniture and lighting inspired by tribal masks and human forms, even straw-roofed booths helped create an exotic, unique milieu. (Lest this commission seem patronizing and degrading, it should be said that Reiss maintained a serious, lifelong interest in black and other minority cultures.)

Joseph Urban's exuberant lounge (*left*) for the (now demolished) Gibson Hotel in Cincinnati, Ohio, was designed in 1928. The furniture has a sturdy Arts and Crafts-cum-Vienna Secession look to it, but the walls were covered with a jubilant floral and butterfly design, echoed somewhat quietly on the chairs' upholstery.

Streamlined curves, mirrored walls and crisp metal detailing gave the lobby of the Governor Shepherd Apartments in Washington, D.C. (*right*) an elegant yet no-nonsense. functionalist look. The architect of the 1938 structure was Joseph Abel, and the lobby was widely praised in contemporary publications.

The Netherland Plaza Hotel in the Carew Tower, Cincinnati, Ohio, was built in 1931; its architect was Walter W. Ahlschlager, who most likely worked in tandem with interior designer George Unger. Sparkling like a latter-day Versailles is the hotel's Hall of Mirrors (*above*). The ornamental balustrade's floral and Neoclassical devices, as well as those on the elevator gate and wall light (*left*), evince a high-style Parisian Art Deco influence, namely that of the metalworkers Edgar Brandt and Raymond Subes. The delicate armature of the hanging lamps, however, recalls the tendrilled metalwork of Dagobert Peche of the Wiener Werkstätte. Most of the hotel's lighting devices were provided by E. F. Caldwell & Co. The opulent hotel was restored in the 1980s by Rita St Clair, who contributed some contemporary elements, including carpets and upholstery, to the original design.

Marrakesh, with its rich, French-laced Arabic culture, is the site of a splendid Art Deco-era hotel, La Mamounia. Numerous French Art Deco furnishings blend harmoniously with Islamic architectural and design elements in this hotel, which began its glittering life in 1923 (and continues to shine today – it was recently restored by French architect-designer André Paccard). One of its restaurants (*opposite right*) has a smart geometric floor, boldly painted ceiling and stepped glass partitions, while the fountain-adorned, Carrara-marble-clad 'Andalusian Patio' (*opposite below*) is traditionally Moorish, albeit duly stylized. Among its various suites are numerous unabashedly French-Moderne bedrooms. The one illustrated here is a mélange of 1920s Paris forms (headboard, table, chair) and native motifs (the bazaar scene over the bed). (*opposite left*).

Resort hotels on Britain's coast often struck Art Deco themes both inside and out. Burgh Island, off the coast of South Devon, dates from 1929 and was (still is) an exclusive, secluded refuge. Its Palm Court (*left*) features the huge Peacock Dome overhead, and wicker chairs, Moderne mirrors and abundant potted plants below. More Modernist and less precious was the 1932-33 Morecombe Hotel in Lancashire, designed by Oliver Hill. Eric Ravilious's huge mural depicting Morning, Noon and Night curved around the restaurant's wall (*below*) and the no-nonsense, tubular-metal furniture was mostly designed by Hill.

The **1929-30 refurbishment of Claridge's**, the London hotel, was supervised by Oswald P. Milne. The dome-topped vestibule (*above*) was painted yellow; over its lacquered-black doors were cheerful floral roundels by Mary S. Lea. Its Wilton carpet was designed by Marion Dorn, as was the massive beige and brown rug in the peach-hued reception area. Overhead was a skylight with a charming aeroplane design (by the Birmingham Guild of Handicraft) and along the sides were tall stepped mirrors, wrought-iron light fixtures and chairs covered with smart Moderne fabric (*above right*). The central recess featured a silvered-metal flower and bird motif against black glass. London's Strand Palace Hotel (*right*) was designed in 1929-30 by Oliver P. Bernard. Its remarkable foyer was a dazzling essay in geometry and light.

The elegant front entrance to Claridge's Hotel, London (*left*), is classic Art Deco *c.* 1930. Illumination is provided by a massive chandelier (reflected in the blue glass-enhanced mirror), a wrought-iron standard lamp, two fixtures high above the black door and, sheltered in a glossy black niche on the right, a Lalique glass base supporting a Moderne deer-amid-foliage sculpture by Oswald Milne. Virtually the same elements appear on the opposite side of the entry hall.

An opulent, classical hotel interior is the so-called Silver Entrance of London's Park Lane Hotel (*below*), whose architect was Henry Tanner and designer Kenneth Anns. Dating from 1927, this magical space is dominated by an exotic-cum-neoclassical mural and handsome floriated metalwork, both on the balustrades and on the armatures enclosing fat cylinders of light. The silver-painted sofa and chairs are original.

Several 1930s London hotels featured outstanding Art Deco interiors, and today some of these spaces remain relatively unchanged, especially the sleek, tiled bathrooms, with smart period light fixtures and chromed-metal details. The dramatic black-tiled example (*opposite below right*) is from the Savoy, the other three from Claridge's. Black borders punctuate the bathroom (*opposite above right*), a pristine space executed largely in cream and white, with a veined-marble floor. Only light hues, notably a blushing apricot shade, mark this bathroom (*opposite above left*), as well as its round and nicely curved mirrors on opposite walls (note the clock). The marble- and mirror-sheathed model (*opposite below left*) is in fact contemporary, but contains echoes of earlier rooms. It too is highlighted with dark borders (here in a bold architectonic pattern) and illuminated by lights set in chromed-metal fittings.

The 50th-storey theatre of New York's Chanin Building was called 'the world's highest auditorium' by a contemporary press release. Its foyer (*above*) was filled with comfortable seats, handsome light fittings, a stepped fireplace and, like its lobby, an array of striking metalwork. Note especially the fire screen, with its cat's-tail motif, and the express-elevator gate on the right.

This view of the extensive marble and metal lobby of Manhattan's Empire State Building (*right*) presents a crisp, stepped space, nicely complementing its massive stone, aluminium and nickel exterior (Shreve, Lamb & Harmon, 1931). There is an abundance of horizontals balancing the soaring verticals, and the floor has a zigzag motif echoing the ripples of the mezzanine and railing just above it.

The Johnson Wax Building in Racine, Wisconsin, designed and furnished by Frank Lloyd
Wright in the late 1930s, was probably the premier Modernist workplace in America. The
building featured a harmonious assortment of curves, ovals and circles, especially in its Great
Workroom, where the high ceiling was seemingly supported by a mass of giant golf-tee-shaped
piers. The original metal furniture was painted dark salmon-russet, a shade that appeared
throughout the edifice (intended by the architect to harmonize with the bricks of the exterior).

The gleaming metal and marble lobby of 275 Madison Avenue (*left*) (designed in 1931 by Kenneth Franzheim and recently refurbished) contains a wealth of Art Deco touches. Among these are the continuous chevron pattern on the floor, the lighting fixtures along the lifts in the background, and the massive metal-sheathed and -banded fluted column in the foreground. (The colour scheme of the recessed ceiling area is not original.)

Famous for its exterior's shimmering pinnacle and automobile-related decorations, Manhattan's Chrysler Building (1927-30, by William Van Alen) also features a stunning lobby (*below*), with *rouge flambé* marble walls, ornamental metalwork by Oscar Bach, a ceiling fresco by Edward Trumbull and banks of exotic-wood lifts, their outer doors sheathed with the Tyler Company's unique METYL'-WOOD veneers in papyrus-like plant forms.

One of the most splendid Art Deco interiors in a commercial building is the 1929-32 Daily Express Building's Reception Hall (*opposite*) in Fleet Street, London, designed by Robert Atkinson and admired by John Betjeman for its 'wonderful rippling confections of metal'. Lighting fixtures, balustrades and other decorative and structural elements are sheathed in white and yellow metal, and on the wall is a relief panel by Eric Aumonier representing a female 'Empire' and her subjects.

Henry J. McGill designed the Church of the Most Precious Blood (*left*) in Astoria, New York. Like an ecclesiastical skyscraper with soaring fluted and stepped arches, the early 1930s church also featured lighting and stained glass with stylized motifs and architectonic elements of the Art Deco variety.

Several British church interiors were conceived in the Modernist vein. Francis X. Velarde's St. Gabriel, Blackburn (*below*), made a strong contemporary statement in 1933, with a chromium reredos shaped like a cross within a high, stepped arch, and cylindrical-tub lectern and pulpit. Its ceiling lights, metal-framed cones of graduated size, were similarly dramatic.

In St. Helier, Jersey, René Lalique, along with British architect A.B. Grayson, designed a new interior for the Victorian church of St. Matthew (*left*) in 1934. Lalique's glass contributions included the new high altar, reredos, altar rail, side walls surrounding the vestry, a smaller chapel and altar, a water font and windows. A lovely refuge of crystalline purity and splendour, St. Matthew's is dominated by the massive illuminated-glass reredos (a cross flanked by two pillars), the three parts of which are decorated at the top with moulded blossoms of the Regal lily, or 'Jersey lily'. The small Lady Chapel has a reredos comprising tall relief panels of angels (*above left*); the detail (*above*) shows part of a wall screen and window.

CHAPTER 6

THE ART DECO INTERIOR REVIVED
RENEWAL AND RESTORATION IN THE 1970s AND 1980s

By the late 1960s, a number of museum curators as well as art dealers were beginning to appreciate the talents of Art Deco designers. The Musée des Arts Décoratifs' exhibition, Les Années 1925, set the stage in Paris in 1966. Then there were the books, foremost among them Bevis Hillier's *Art Deco of the 20s and 30s* (1968), which extolled the variety, virtues and vagaries of the style. The term 'Art Deco' came into popular usage in the early 1970s, and by the middle of the decade a full-fledged revival of Art Deco was in process. Of course, many Modernist designs of the 1920s and 1930s – tubular-steel furniture and especially the designs of Le Corbusier, Mies van der Rohe and Breuer – had never gone out of fashion and had in fact become timeless classics almost as soon as they were introduced.

The 1970s, however, after the hotch-potch eclecticism of the previous decade, witnessed a resurgence of interest in high-style Art Deco as well, especially in the works of Ruhlmann, Dunand, Poiret and Süe et Mare. All these designers merited one- (or, in the case of the latter pair, two-) man shows, these in addition to their representation in one or more of several significant exhibitions: Art Deco, at the Finch College Museum of Art in New York (1970), the Minneapolis Institute of Art's The World of Art Deco (1971), the travelling Canadian Exhibition, Art Deco 1925-35 (1975) and the Cinquantenaire de l'Exposition de 1925 at the Musée des Arts Décoratifs in Paris (albeit a year or so late, 1976-77). Elsewhere, exhibitions were being mounted of regional Art Deco design, such as The Thirties, a show at London's Hayward Gallery in 1979-80, Art Deco aus Frankreich in Frankfurt-am-Main's Museum für Kunsthandwerk in 1975 and Die Zwanziger Jahre, at Zürich's Kunstgewerbemuseum in 1973. More recently, At Home in Manhattan, Modern Decorative Arts 1925 to the Depression, was presented at the Yale University Art Gallery (1983), and New York's Whitney Museum of American Art showed the ambitious High Styles, Twentieth-Century American Design (1985-86), both of which highlighted many examples of Art Deco, especially in the context of interior design. In addition, auction sales of famous collections increased the public's awareness of the style, foremost among these the Hôtel Drouot's sale of the 'Ancienne Collection Jacques Doucet' in 1972 and Sotheby's auction of the Maharajah of Indore's magnificent Modernist furnishings in Monaco in 1980.

The homes of famous collectors of Art Deco emerged on the pages of magazines, among them Yves Saint Laurent, Karl Lagerfeld, Barbra Streisand and Elton John, and before too long reproductions of Art Deco furniture were being made. Some of these, such as Eileen Gray's 'Bibendum' and 'Transat' chairs, were made by authorized licenced firms with official approval, but others were very much 'in-the-style-of' imitations, inferior in construction, but far more affordable in price for the aspirational general public, who were now largely familiar with the term 'Art Deco'. Imitation 1920s design appeared in profusion, applied to a plethora of tacky ceramic figurines and any knick-knack with a geometric motif on it was termed 'Deco'.

The revival of the Art Deco style, besides being manifested in the collecting of objects from that period, was characterized by modern adaptations of elements of Art Deco, graphics probably being the first category of art to 'seize the Déco' and capitalize on Cassandresque and Edward McKnight Kauffer-like typefaces and images. Indeed, Erté, the Russian-born illustrator, was still producing work in a style not far removed from that in which he had worked a half-century earlier, so how could he not but succeed in the renaissance? Fashions from the period were again in vogue (being worn as well as exhibited in museums), 1920s and 1930s movies were screened religiously in repertory cinemas – and 1970s and 1980s films were featuring streamlined or elegant 1920s and 1930s sets – revivals of old musicals and revues were presented in Deco-style settings. Even contemporary artists, such as Frank Stella and Roy Lichtenstein, displayed a certain recognition of *le style 1925* in their works, not to mention hundreds of known and anonymous artists employing Art Deco motifs in designs for book covers, packaging, greeting cards, wrapping papers, textiles and posters.

The Art Deco interior was by no means neglected in this mass revival. Whole interiors – whether 'actual' or re-created – featured in many of the Art Deco exhibitions being presented around the world, and, best of all, the interiors of many authentic Art Deco buildings – those which had not been demolished or renovated beyond legitimate resurrection – were being dusted off, painted, re-gilded or otherwise restored, with resounding success and sound approval from both the experts and general public. Especially in the United States, civic- and aesthetic-minded Art Deco preservation leagues, conservancies and societies – in places like Tulsa, New York, Miami, Indianapolis and Hartford – were formed, and were instrumental in both conserving and restoring these structures and educating the public as to their value and beauty. Many exteriors and interiors from the Art Deco period were even declared national or regional landmarks, and thus could not be disastrously modernized or wholly destroyed.

Cinemas, theatres, hotels, cafés, restaurants, even post offices and town halls were spruced up and returned to their original splendour, or close approximations of it. Unfortunately, some were badly restored, with the colours and new accessories chosen completely wrong for the original setting, but many were lovingly, painstakingly rejuvenated to remarkable likenesses of their old, vibrant selves. But the Art Deco revival did not just entail looking reverently at the objects, places, fashions, graphics and films of the past and then attempting to religiously re-create period details. It also attracted decided-

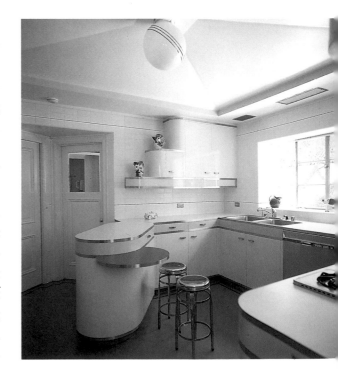

This sleek Californian kitchen has all the modern conveniences, but is still evocative of the 1930s with its nicely streamlined curves. Chrome and red highlights enliven the mostly pastel space (the round shelf that pivots out from the cabinet is a practical touch of the type Eileen Gray introduced in the 1920s). Buzz Yudell designed the kitchen in the 1980s.

ly contemporary, and not stubbornly retrospective, designers – of both objects and whole interiors – who borrowed elements from Art Deco designs, shapes, materials, motifs and colour combinations to create vivid, undeniably modern interiors. Authentic period pieces might even be mixed with contemporary, complementary and homage-paying pieces to make a new hybrid design statement. Indeed, the Art Deco interior in the 1970s and 1980s was a horse of many colours: from purist to pastiche, fable to facsimile, unabashedly regal to embarrassingly retro-kitsch. It appeared in television quiz and chat shows, snack bars and brasseries, City banks and country hotels, department stores and discothèques.

Art Deco interiors in the recent past, i.e., the last two decades, can be said to fall into three general, but by no means finite and clear-cut, categories, each with related offshoots, exceptions and aberrations. First, there are the obvious renovations and refurbishments of authentic Art Deco-period interiors. These can either be piece-by-piece re-creations, or very close approximations, of an original setting, such as the exhibit of the rooms designed by Armand-Albert Rateau for Jeanne Lanvin and re-constituted in the Musée des Arts Décoratifs in Paris today. Or, belonging equally to this general category, is the usage of an Art Deco interior as a firm basis on which to add elements which were not part of the original setting. These elements might be authentic 1920s and 1930s pieces or present-day reproductions, or they might be contemporary designs with an Art Deco feel or flavour, or merely complementary modern (in some cases, Post-Modern) pieces which evoke an earlier period or are at least sympathetic to, even harmonious with, the past. Into this extensive category fall such interiors as those of the Omni Starrett Netherlands Plaza Hotel in Cincinnati, Ohio, recently restored by Rita St. Clair, and those of the Raymond McGrath-designed Surrey House, St. Ann's Hill, restored both inside and out by the London architectural and design firm, Davis & Bayne. Likewise, Theo Crosby, of the multimedia London design firm, Pentagram, restored the interiors of the 1930s London headquarters of the Unilever corporation in the 1980s, making use of many of the already-present architectural elements, but adding his own exuberant, colourful Art Deco-style touches (especially lighting fixtures and ornamental metalwork and leaded glass) to make a unique contemporary statement in a living design language.

The second general category of Art Deco interior is largely the domain of the private collector, who has acquired genuine, significant pieces of Art Deco furniture and period objects and mixed-and-matched them – sometimes with older antique or newer contemporary pieces – to come up with a distinctive, evocative setting. Numerous Parisian houses and apartments – those of fashion designers Yves Saint Laurent and Karl Lagerfeld in the late 1970s, for example (since dismantled) – became living, breathing *hommages au style*

1925, as did the rooms of a number of major collectors in London, New York and Los Angeles among them. Of course, a multitude of pastiches and mixes can fit into this section – hybrid and international mélanges of French and English, or French and American, or high-style Parisian and Modernist Parisian, elements. Indeed, the interior designed in the true spirit of Art Deco can take on many guises, some pure and refined, others a hotch-potch bordering on kitsch.

The last type of interior is one that is almost entirely contemporary, but contains furniture, accessories and architectural elements which are obviously modern (often Post-Modern) but nonetheless recall, or make references to, Art Deco. The creations of American architects Charles Jencks and Michael Graves and Parisian furniture and interior designer Andrée Putman (whose firm, Ecart, is also authorized to reproduce works by Eileen Gray, Pierre Chareau, Jean-Michel Frank and other Modernists) fit into this category, as do some interiors dominated by the colourful furniture, objects and fabrics designed and manufactured by the Milan-based Memphis group (of which Ettore Sottsass, Jr. was the most significant figure, but whose other designers included Michele de Lucchi, George J. Sowden, Matteo Thun, Nathalie du Pasquier and Michael Graves). Memphis pieces have also been combined with sympathetic early designs – Josef Hoffmann sofas and chairs, for instance, reproduced today by the German firm Wittmann.

Perhaps more numerous than any of the above types of interiors are those incorporating Art Deco or Art Deco-style pieces into them. For instance, the elegant, light-wood-veneered furniture or bold 'Stanmore' bed or 'Plaza' dressing table of Michael Graves, the craftsman-made, Ruhlmann-inspired masterworks of American furniture designer Wendell Castle (whose organic, laminated wood settees of the late 1960s Studio Craft Movement evoked the curvilinearity of Art Nouveau), and the sofas and chairs of Nicky Noyes – fat, comfortable forms covered with boldly hued neo-Deco fabrics – can easily blend with authentic Art Deco pieces to create an Art Deco-style atmosphere that is neither imitative nor pastiche. Likewise, contemporary reproductions of furniture designed by Le Corbusier and Perriand, Marcel Breuer, Alvar Aalto, Eliel Saarinen or Eileen Gray can comfortably embellish an interior of predominantly Post-Modern design. Indeed, the variations on and permutations of the Art Deco interior in the 1970s and 1980s were many and diverse, and surely the next decade – and beyond – will witness further evocations of this recent era.

Warm tones and exotic touches distinguish the handsome living room in this Paris apartment decorated in the Art Deco style in the early 1970s. With its tribal stool (in the foreground), mass of animal-skin-covered pillows, and metal and lacquered vases by Jean Dunand, the room pays homage to 1920s Paris, specifically to the Moderne tastes of Jacques Doucet.

This 1970s apartment was decorated in an Art Deco vein with bold contemporary touches. The highly rectilinear, much-mirrored bathroom (*opposite*) has rich red and black highlights – on the stool, the carpet, even the powder compacts displayed on the lower right. The bedroom (*above*) contains a sharkskin-top Ruhlmann desk, an André Groult mirror and bold abstract carpet; its modern components – the Italian Brionvega stereo (a 1965 Achille Castiglioni design), the standard lamp on the left, the nocturnal painting – harmonize nicely with the strong period elements.

The Venice apartment of art dealer Carlo Medioli (*above*) blends 1920s classics with both antique and contemporary objects. The dining room, with its black-lacquered, mirror-topped table by Ruhlmann, and tubular-metal chairs and tea trolley, also contains a modern black-lacquered cabinet (on the right), an antique chandelier and, on the table, dinnerware of Medioli's own design (the plates reproduce period engravings of Italian villas).

Some of the common stylized motifs of the Art Deco period – the leaping deer and giant blossoms, for instance – appear in this 1970s English sitting room (*left*). The pedestal table and rug under it provide authentic Moderne touches, as do some of the ceramics on the updated-skyscraper-style cabinet on the right.

The Paris flat of *parfumeuse* **Hélène Rochas** is a stylish mix of three centuries of classic French design, including eighteenth-century masterworks by Tilliard and Jacob, lavish French Empire pieces and Art Deco creations, all of which blend with a superb collection of modern art. In the blue-lacquered room (*below*) there is furniture by Pierre Chareau and Eileen Gray, and on the mantelpiece a group of enamelled-metal vases by Camille Fauré. The warm-hued boudoir-sitting area (*left*) features a Daum lamp, an ivory- and sharkskin-adorned Ruhlmann dressing table and chair, and a tooled-leather cabinet by Clément Mère.

One of the most successful production designers in both film and theatre, and a self-acknowledged lover of Art Deco since the late 1960s, is Tony Walton. His sets for Ken Russell's Art Deco extravaganza, *The Boy Friend* (1970), set the stage for a litany of projects that have presented some of the brightest, most exuberant glimpses into this vibrant past. The dramatic black and gold boudoir (*opposite below*), a deliberate exaggeration of high-style Paris, is not unlike the set for *Women Love Diamonds* (see page 158). In the Broadway musical *Chicago*, the look was crisply mirrored and metallic, with a hint of stylized flowers, as the model for a bedroom scene (with musical accompaniment!) shows (*opposite above*). The rendering (*above*) for the Broadway play *Social Security* is elegant and urbane, with dark-lacquered curves and a deft combination of furniture both Moderne and later (like the 1956 fibreglass armchair by Eero Saarinen on the left).

Architect Michael Graves created these two showrooms for the Sunar furniture company of Norwalk, Connecticut (which produces some of his own designs). In Chicago (*above*) the massive pink and blue pillars proclaim Post-Modernism in both palette and form, but the thick cylinders, emphasized by 'capitals' of vertical lines, recall some of the simple yet bold architectural elements of early Modernist interiors. The 1979 New York showroom (*left*), on the other hand, makes use of subtle, stepped elements and pale, graduated tones to effect a harmonious geometric essay.

The 'Astoria' bathroom suite (*opposite*), from the British firm B.C. Sanitan, is a generously proportioned late 1980s room with a deliberately Art Deco feel. The stepped bathroom fixtures, the architectonic black-striped wall mirror, the light over the tub and the two period-style works of art (one a reproduction of Picasso's *Le Train Bleu*, originally a backdrop for a Ballets Russes production) all contribute to its period flavour.

In the early 1980s redecoration of London's 1931 Unilever House, Pentagram designer Theo
Crosby made use of many of the period architectural elements, adding to them his own
colourful Art Deco-style touches. The stained- and frosted-glass windows leading to its
Thames Restaurant (*opposite below*) are covered with geometric designs and closely resemble
the early leaded-glass windows of Frank Lloyd Wright. Crosby's bold geometric lighting
fixtures are one of his trademarks. They also enliven other Pentagram projects, such as the
1987 NMB Bank in Bijlmermeer, Amsterdam, famous for its Ton Alberts-designed exterior –
ten jagged towers comprising a crooked S-shaped form. The lobby's fluted white pillars
(*opposite above left*) are topped by tall illuminated leaded-glass panels, while a restaurant
(*above*) is lit by three-dimensional triangles of light attached to arms emerging from giant
columns. The office of London solicitor Forsyte-Kerman (*opposite above right*) features
exuberant stained-glass windows, lighting and, as in Unilever House, stellate forms sprouting
from marble-clad columns and seeming to burst on to the ceiling.

THAMES RESTAURANT

The 1930s Derry & Toms' building in London's Kensington High Street was transformed by
Barbara Hulanicki into her Deco-revival retail emporium Biba in 1973 (*above*). From its
mirrored and chromed architectonic display cases to its stylish gold and black packaging,
1920s-inspired motifs and forms were the order of the day. The ripple-sided settees, their bold,
geometric-patterned upholstery matching the carpet and curtains, can be seen today as Art
Deco revival laced with psychedelic Pop.

French designer Andrée Putman designed a timeless model apartment in New York's Metropolitan Tower in 1986, the whole a harmonious, space-saving exercise in black and white, with most furnishings by Putman's firm, Ecart, but designed originally in 1920s and 1930s Paris. Two Eileen Gray 'Transat' chairs sit on a Gray carpet in the sitting room (*above*), while the dining area beyond features a J. H. Lartigue table and Mallet-Stevens chairs. The tall lamp on the left is by Fortuny, the dark grey leather sofa in the foreground by Jean-Michel Frank and Adolphe Chanaux. The Tower's private dining room (*right*), designed by Bill Derman, has numerous period overtones, such as the chequerboard designs on the mirrored wall panels and round tables, and the metal-banded, wood columns and pilasters.

British designer Pauline Hoffman created several handsome interiors for a London bank in the late 1980s, partly inspired by the Wiener Werkstätte. One room (*left*) features two modern reproductions (by Wittmann) of a Josef Hoffmann armchair, originally made in 1911 for the Haus Koller; these are upholstered in black with white outlines. The reception area (*below left*) also contains reproduction Viennese furniture: the boxy 'Cabinett' double-seat bench and chair on the right. The red and cream shades of their upholstery (also vintage Vienna) are echoed in the contemporary architectonic tapestry sheathing the pillar on the left, and the gouache on the wall; both are by Juliette Barclay.

This sitting room (*below*) **is in St. Ann's Hill**, a 1937 Surrey house designed by Modernist architect Raymond McGrath. Present owners Phil and Sharron Manzanera opted to furnish this dramatic, rounded space with new pieces sympathetic to the period setting and palette (the original colour scheme was pastel pink and green). London architect Davis & Bayne, along with Fred Baier and Chris Rose, helped to realize the finished product, with its plush seating and wedge-shaped tables; Nicholas French's circular rug enhances the harmonious effect.

A cosy and comfortable mélange of various 1920s and 1930s pieces coalesces into an eminently practical space in Louise Levin's Westport, Connecticut, home. In the bright kitchen (*opposite*) are gleaming chrome accessories by Chase Brass & Copper of Waterbury, Connecticut, and Eliel Saarinen's futuristic spherical urn and tray (made by the International Silver Company of Meriden).

ACKNOWLEDGMENTS

My first, and warmest, thanks must go to Frank Murphy, who endured my researching and writing *Art Deco Interiors* for well over a year and helped me through many of the hard parts; as did my mother, Helen Bayer, who gave me much long-distance aid and support.

Friends, colleagues, even strangers I had never met before – some I never *did* meet, but hope to – proved extremely helpful, particularly in terms of locating photographs. I would especially like to single out Mark Waller and Martine de Cervens of Galerie Moderne, London, for letting me have access to a rich library; Roslyn Willett, who was so generous and hospitable to me in New York, and Marian Appellof, Michael Goldman and Pamela Ross, other New York friends who provided valuable help. A special thank you to Tony Walton, who, despite being so busy with a new Broadway show, sent me a wonderful selection of photographs to look at – I only wish we had room for more of them in the book!

To the following people in London, I would like to express my gratitude: Peter Aprahamian, Gertrude Buckman, Lee Curtis, Allen Eyles, Julian Feary, Philippe Garner, Roger Lubbock, Davydd Myburgh, Paul Orssich, Julie Anne and Nick Rhodes, Lucinda Buxton and Rosemary Ashbee at the Savoy Hotel, Paul Davis of Davis & Bayne, Mary Godwin at the Design Museum, Andrew Mead at the Architectural Press, Michael D. Millar of Millar & Harris, Amelia Gatacre and Debbie Richardson at Pentagram Design, Karen Tooth at Unilever, the slide librarians at the Architectural Association and the staff of the Greater London Photograph Library. Elsewhere in Great Britain, thanks to Rudolph Kenna, Andrew L. Edwards, Pauline Hoffman and Roger Sears.

Further thanks go to, in New York: Molly and Norman McGrath, Howard and Ronald Mandelbaum, Robert Cashey, Kent M. Swig, Alastair Duncan, Margaret Civetta, Jacqueline Damian, Sjoerd Doting, Barbara Friedland, Leo Orenstein and Cathy Peck; elsewhere in the United States, Donna Cettei, Diane Hart, Andrea Russo and Michael Bingham, Mary Moore Jacoby at the Virginia Museum of Fine Arts, Michael Houlihan of Hedrich-Blessing and Alan Prisus; in Dublin, Tom Kiernan; in Paris, Ariane Garnier, Jean-Loup Charmet, Jérôme Darblay, Kathleen Chamousset at RAPHO, M. & Mme. Lucien Hervé, Geneviève de Tarragon at Edimédia, and Françoise Mommessin and Françoise Durand at Agence T.O.P.; and in Amsterdam, Frank den Oudsten, and Gea and Abdou el-Moutamid.

Further afield, I must thank two Australian correspondents: Robert Hill of The Paragon in Katoomba, New South Wales, and Daniel Thomas, Director of the Art Gallery of South Australia in Adelaide.

I know I have left out many individuals, companies and organizations, so I would like to extend a blanket thanks to all those other people and sources (some of which do appear in the Picture Credits).

PATRICIA BAYER, London

GALLERIES AND MUSEUMS

Many of the interiors written about and illustrated in this book are long gone, but several museums, period houses and other buildings throughout the world still include elements of the Art Deco interior, whether by replicating actual 1920s and 1930s rooms, by creating rooms that 'are in the style of' period Art Deco interiors or simply featuring superb Art Deco collections, though not necessarily in room settings. Of course, there are countless cinemas, theatres, town halls, hotels, office buildings, railroad stations and so on that still exist in (usually refurbished) Art Deco splendour. A list of such buildings, however, would be far too extensive to include here, but they are not too difficult to find, especially in the United States, where architectural preservation organizations have been as eager to preserve or restore good twentieth-century buildings as well as those of earlier vintage.

This list of galleries and museums is by no means an exhaustive one; rather, it is just a special selection of places well worth visiting to gain further insight into the interior design of the 1920s and 1930s.

UNITED STATES

The Metropolitan Museum of Art
Fifth Avenue and 82nd Street
New York, New York 10028

The Museum of Modern Art
11 West 53rd Street
New York, New York 10019

R.M.S. Queen Mary
Pier J
Long Beach, California 90803

**Barnsdall House Museum
(Hollyhock House)**
4800 Hollywood Boulevard
Barnsdall Park
Los Angeles, California 90029
(a Frank Lloyd Wright house)

Virginia Museum of Fine Arts
Boulevard and Grove Avenue
Richmond, Virginia 23221

The Brooklyn Museum
Eastern Parkway and Washington Avenue
Brooklyn, New York 11238

Cranbrook Academy of Art Museum
500 Lone Pine Road
Bloomfield Hills, Michigan 48013

The Mitchell Wolfson Jr. Collection of Decorative & Propaganda Arts
Miami-Dade Community College
New World Center
300 NE Second Avenue
Miami, Florida 33132

EUROPE

Victoria & Albert Museum
Cromwell Road
London SW7

Geffrye Museum
Kingsland Road
London E2

Brighton Museum and Art Gallery
Church Street
Brighton BN1 1UE

Musée des Arts Décoratifs
107-109 rue de Rivoli
75001 Paris

Kunstindustri Museum (Museum of Decorative Art)
68 Bredgade
DK 1260 Copenhagen K

Österreichisches Museum für angewandte Kunst
Stubenring 5
A-1010 Vienna

The Rietveld Schröder House
50 Prins Hendriklaan
Utrecht

ELSEWHERE

Tokyo Metropolitan Teien Art Museum
21-9 Shirokanedai, 5-Chome
Minato-ku
Tokyo 108

Musée des Arts Décoratifs
Le Château Dufresne
Pie IX & Sherbrooke
Montréal, Québec H3C 3P3

BIBLIOGRAPHY

Although there may be some books arranged in the following categories whose contents somewhat overlap another category, their prime concerns lie within the heading they appear under.

GENERAL

Albrecht, Donald, *Designing Dreams, Modern Architecture in the Movies*, New York, 1986; London, 1987.
Anscombe, Isabelle, *A Woman's Touch, Women in Design from 1860 to the Present*, London and New York, 1984.
Applegate, Joseph, *The Book of Furniture and Decoration: Period and Modern*, New York, 1936.
Arwas, Victor, *Art Deco*, London and New York, 1980.
Atwell, David, *Cathedrals of the Movies*, London, 1980.

Banham, Reyner, *Theory and Design in the First Machine Age*, London, 1960.
Battersby, Martin, *The Decorative Twenties*, London, 1969 (reprinted 1989).
Battersby, Martin, *The Decorative Thirties*, London, 1971 (reprinted 1989).
Bayer, Patricia, *Art Deco Source Book*, Oxford and New York, 1988.
Brandt, Frederick R., *Late 19th and Early 20th Century Decorative Arts, The Sydney and Frances Lewis Collection in the Virginia Museum of Fine Arts*, Richmond, 1985.
Brinnin, John Malcolm and Gaulin, Kenneth, *The Transatlantic Style*, London, 1988.
Brown, Robert K., *Art Deco Internationale*, New York and London, 1977.
Brunhammer, Yvonne, *The Art Deco Style*, London, 1983; New York, 1984.
Brunhammer, Yvonne, *Cinquantenaire de l'Exposition de 1925*, Paris, 1976.

Cabanne, Pierre, *Encyclopédie Art Déco*, Paris, 1986.

Dean, Barry, *Design Review, Industrial Design 24th Annual*, New York and London, 1978.
Dufrêne, Maurice, *Authentic Art Deco Interiors from the 1925 Paris Exhibition*, Woodbridge, 1989 (reprinted from original 1926 edition).
Duncan, Alastair, *Art Deco*, London, 1988.
Duncan, Alastair (contributing ed.), *Encyclopedia of Art Deco*, London, 1988.

Garner, Philippe (ed.), *The Encyclopedia of Decorative Arts, 1890-1940*, New York and London, 1982 (revised 1989).
Garner, Philippe, *Twentieth-Century Furniture*, Oxford and New York, 1980.

Haslam, Malcolm, *Art Deco*, London, 1987.
Heskett, John, *Industrial Design*, London, 1980.
Hillier, Bevis, *Art Deco of the 20s and 30s*, London and New York, 1968.
Hillier, Bevis, *The Style of the Century 1900-1980*, London and New York, 1983.
Hillier, Bevis, *The World of Art Deco* (exhibition catalogue), New York, 1971.
Hitchcock, Henry-Russell and Johnson, Philip, *The International Style*, London and New York, 1968.
Hunter-Stiebel, Penelope, *20th Century Decorative Arts, The Metropolian Museum of Art Bulletin*, Winter 1979-1980, New York, 1979.

Klein, Dan, *All Colour Book of Art Deco*, London, 1974.
Klein, Dan and Bishop, Margaret, *Decorative Arts 1880-1980*, Oxford, 1986.
Klein, Dan, McClelland, Nancy A. and Haslam, Malcolm, *In the Deco Style*, London, 1987.

Mandelbaum, Howard and Myers, Eric, *Screen Deco, A Celebration of High Style in Hollywood*, New York, 1985.
Maenz, Paul, *Art Deco: 1920-1940*, Cologne, 1974.

Patmore, Derek, *Colour Schemes for the Modern Home*, London, 1933.
Patmore, Derek, *Modern Furnishing and Decorating*, London, 1934.
Pevsner, Nikolaus, *Pioneers of Modern Design from William Morris to Walter Gropius*, New York, 1949; London, 1960.
Pevsner, Nikolaus, *The Sources of Modern Architecture and Design*, New York and London, 1968.

Scarlett, Frank and Townley, Marjorie, *Arts Décoratifs 1925: A Personal Recollection of the Paris Exhibition*, London, 1975.

Teague, Walter Dorwin, *Design This Day, The Technique of Order in the Machine Age*, New York, 1940.

Van de Lemme, Arie, *A Guide to Art Deco Style*, London, 1986.
Veronesi, Giulia, *Into the Twenties: Style and Design 1909-1929*, London, 1958 (published in New York as *Style and Design 1909-1929*, 1968).
Veronesi, Giulia, *Stile 25*, Florence, 1966.

FRENCH ART DECO

Adam, Peter, *Eileen Gray Architect/Designer, A Biography*, New York and London, 1987.

Badovici, Jean, *Harmonies: Intérieurs de Ruhlmann*, Paris, 1924.
Badovici, Jean, *Intérieurs Français*, Paris, 1925.
Badovici, Jean, *Intérieurs de Süe et Mare*, Paris, 1924.
Bayer, Patricia and Waller, Mark, *The Art of René Lalique*, London, 1988.
Bizot, Chantal and Mannoni, Edith, *Mobilier 1900-1925*, Paris, 1978.
Buffet-Challié, Laurence, *Le Moderne Style*, Paris, 1976.

Camard, Florence, *Ruhlmann, Master of Art Deco*, London, 1984.
Clouzot, Henri, *Le Style Moderne dans la décoration moderne*, Paris, 1921.

Deshairs, Léon, *Une Ambassade Française*, Paris, 1925.
Deshairs, Léon, *L'Art Décoratif Français, 1918-25*, Paris, 1925.
Deshairs, Léon, *Exposition des Arts Décoratifs, Paris, 1925, Intérieurs en couleur*, Paris, n.d.
Deshairs, Léon, *L'Hôtel du Collectionneur*, Paris, 1926.
Deshairs, Léon, *Modern French Decorative Art*, London, 1926.
Dufrêne, Maurice, *Intérieurs Français au Salon des Artistes Décorateurs en 1926*, Paris, 1926.
Duncan, Alastair, *Art Deco Furniture, the French Designers*, London and New York, 1984.

Follot, Paul, *Intérieurs Français au Salon des Artistes Décorateurs de 1927*, Paris, 1927.
Foucart, Bruno; Offrey, Charles; Robichon, François and Villers, Claude, *Normandie, Queen of the Seas*, London, 1986.
Fréchet, André, *Intérieurs modernes, mobilier et décoration*, Paris, 1923.
Friedman, Joe, *Inside Paris*, Oxford, 1989.
Fry, Charles Rahn (ed.), *Art Deco Interiors in Color*, New York, 1977.

Kjellberg, Pierre, *Art Déco: Les Maîtres du Mobilier*, Paris, 1981.

Le Corbusier, *Towards a New Architecture*, Paris, 1923; London, 1927.

Lempicka-Foxhall, Baroness Kizette de and Phillips, Charles, *Passion by Design, The Art and Times of Tamara de Lempicka*, Oxford, 1987.

Lesieutre, Alain, *The Spirit and Splendour of Art Deco*, London, 1981.

Lévy, Ed. Albert, *Répertoire du Goût Moderne*, Paris, 1928, 1929.

Menten, Theodore, *The Art Deco Style in Household Objects, Architecture, Sculpture, Graphics, Jewelry*, New York, 1972.

Moussinac, Léon, *Intérieurs*, Paris, 1924, 1925, 1926.

Quenioux, G., *Les Arts Décoratifs*, Paris, 1925.

Robinson, Julian, *The Brilliance of Art Deco*, Sydney, n.d.

Vellay, Marc and Frampton, Kenneth, *Pierre Chareau*, London, 1985.

See also the 13-volume *Rapport Général* of the 1925 Paris Exhibition: *Exposition Internationale des Arts Décoratifs et Industriels Modernes*, Paris, 1927 (reprinted New York, 1927, in a different format).

AMERICAN ART DECO

Appelbaum, Stanley, *The New York World's Fair 1939/1940 in Photographs by Richard Wurts and Others*, New York, 1977.

Bush, Donald J., *The Streamlined Decade*, New York, 1975.

Cerwinske, Laura, *Tropical Deco: The Architecture and Design of Old Miami Beach*, New York, 1981.

Chanin, Irwin S., *A Romance with the City*, New York, 1982.

Clark, Robert Judson et al., *Design in America: The Cranbrook Vision 1925-1950* (exhibition catalogue), New York, 1983.

Corn, Joseph J. and Horrigan, Brian, *Yesterday's Tomorrows: Past Visions of the American Future*, New York, 1984.

Cucchiella, So., *Baltimore Deco: An Architectural Survey of Art Deo in Baltimore*, Baltimore, 1984.

Darling, Sharon, *Chicago Furniture Art, Craft and Industry 1833-1933*, Chicago, 1984.

Davies, Karen, *At Home in Manhattan: Modern Decorative Arts 1925 to the Depression* (exhibition catalogue), New Haven, 1983.

Duncan, Alastair, *American Art Deco*, New York and London, 1986.

Ferriss, Hugh, *The Metropolis of Tomorrow*, New York, 1929.

Frankl, Paul T., *Form and Re-Form*, New York, 1930.

Frankl, Paul T., *Machine-Made Leisure*, New York, 1932.

Frankl, Paul T., *New Dimensions, The Decorative Arts of Today in Words and Pictures*, New York, 1928 (reprinted 1976).

Gebhard, David and Von Breton, Harriette, *Kem Weber: The Moderne in Southern California, 1920-1941* (exhibition catalogue), Santa Barbara, 1969.

Gebhard, David and Von Breton, Harriette, *L.A. in the Thirties, 1931-1941*, Salt Lake City, 1975.

Gebhard, David and Winter, Robert, *Tulsa Art Deco: An Architectural Era, 1925-1942*, Oklahoma, 1980.

Glory, June, *Art Deco in Indianapolis*, Indianapolis, 1980.

Goldberger, Paul, *The City Observed: New York, A Guide to the Architecture of Manhattan*, New York, 1979.

Goldberger, Paul, *The Skyscraper*, New York, 1982.

Greif, Martin, *Depression Modern: The Thirties Style in America*, New York, 1975.

Hanks, David, *The Decorative Designs of Frank Lloyd Wright*, New York, 1979.

Hanks, David and Toher, Jennifer, *Donald Deskey, Decorative Designs and Interiors*, New York, 1987.

Hanks, David A., *Innovative Furniture in America from 1800 to the Present Day*, New York, 1981.

Harrison, Helen, *Dawn of a New Day: The New York World's Fair 1939-1940* (exhibition catalogue), New York, 1980.

Hennessey, William J., *Russel Wright: American Designer* (exhibition catalogue), Cambridge, Mass., 1983.

Kaplan, Donald and Bellink, Alan, *Classic Diners of the Northeast*, Boston and London, 1980.

Kingsbury, Martha, *Age of the Thirties – The Pacific Northwest*, Seattle, 1972.

Krinsky, Carol Herselle, *Rockefeller Center*, Oxford, London and New York, 1978.

Meikle, Jeffrey L., *Twentieth Century Limited: Industrial Design in America 1925-1939*, Philadelphia, 1979.

Pilgrim, Dianne, *The Machine Age in America 1918-1941* (exhibition catalogue), Brooklyn, 1986.

Pulos, Arthur J., *American Design Ethic*, Cambridge, Mass., 1982.

Robinson, Cervin and Bletter, Rosemarie Haag, *Skyscraper Architecture: Art Deco New York*, New York, 1985.

Shepherd Gallery, *Winold Reiss 1886-1953 Centennial Exhibition* (catalogue), New York, 1986.

University of Cincinnati, *Art Deco and the Cincinnati Union Terminal*, Cincinnati, 1973.

Varian, Elayne H., *American Art Deco Architecture* (exhibition catalogue), New York, 1974.

Weber, Eva, *Art Deco in America*, New York, 1985.

Weiss, Peg, *The Art Deco Environment*, Syracuse, NY, 1976.

Westerman, Nada and Wessel, Jean, *American Design Classics*, New York, 1986.

Whiffen, Marcus and Breeze, Carla, *Pueblo Deco: The Art Deco Architecture of the Southwest*, Albuquerque, NM, 1984.

Whitney Museum of American Art, *High Styles: Twentieth-Century American Design* (exhibition catalogue), New York, 1985.

Wirz, Hans and Striner, Richard, *Washington Deco: Art Deco in the Nation's Capital*, Washington, D.C., 1984.

BRITISH ART DECO

Arts Council of Great Britain, *Thirties, British Art and Design before the War* (exhibition catalogue), London, 1979.

Cantacuzino, S., *Wells Coates*, London, 1978.

Cooper, Jackie (ed.), *Mackintosh Architecture*, London and New York, 1977 and 1984.

Dean, David, *Architecture of the 1930s, Recalling the English Scene*, New York, 1983.

BIBLIOGRAPHY

Friedman, Joe, *Inside London*, Oxford, 1988.

Goodden, Susanna, *At the Sign of the Fourposter, A History of Heal's*, London, 1984.

Hitchcock, Henry-Russell and Bauer, C., *Modern Architecture in England*, New York, 1937 (reprinted 1969).

Kenna, Rudolph, *Glasgow Art Deco*, Glasgow, 1985.

MacCarthy, Fiona, *All Things Bright and Beautiful: Design in Britain 1930 to Today*, London, 1972 (revised 1979).
McGrath, Raymond and Frost, A. C., *Glass in Architecture and Decoration*, London, 1937 (reprinted 1961).
McGrath, Raymond, *Twentieth Century Houses*, London, 1934.

Sharp, Dennis, Benton, Tim and Cole, Barbie Campbell, *PEL and Tubular Steel Furniture of the Thirties*, London, 1977.
Stamp, Gavin (ed.), *Britain in the Thirties*, London, n.d. (Architectural Design Profile 24).

Ward, Mary and Neville, *Home in the 20s and 30s*, London, n.d.

OTHER EUROPEAN ART DECO CONCURRENT DESIGN

Blaser, Werner, *Mies van der Rohe, Furniture and Interiors*, London, 1982.
Bossaglia, Rosanna, *Il 'Deco' Italiano: Fisionomia delo Stilo 1925 in Italia*, Milan, 1975.

Leidelmeijer, Frans and van der Cingel, Daan, *Art Nouveau en Art Deco in Nederland*, The Netherlands, 1983.

Naylor, Gillian, *The Bauhaus*, London, 1968.

Overy, Paul, *De Stijl*, London, 1968.
Overy, Paul; Büller, Lenneke; den Oudsten, Frank and Mulder, Bertus, *The Rietveld Schröder House*, Houten, 1988.

PARCO, *Czechoslovakia Cubism: The World of Architecture, Furniture and Craft*, Tokyo, 1984.

Schweiger, Werner J., *Wiener Werkstätte, Design in Vienna 1903-1932*, London, 1984.
Sembach, Klaus-Jürgen, *Into the Thirties: Style and Design, 1927-1934*, London, 1972.
Sembach, Klaus-Jürgen, *Style 1930*, New York, 1971.

Varnedoe, Kirk, *Vienna 1900: Art, Architecture & Design* (exhibition catalogue), New York, 1986.
Vergo, Peter, *Art in Vienna 1898-1918*, London, 1975.

Whitford, Frank, *Bauhaus*, London, 1984.
Wilk, Christopher, *Marcel Breuer, Furniture and Interiors*, New York, 1981.
Wingler, Hans M., *Bauhaus*, Cambridge, Mass., 1969.
Wit, Wim de (gen. ed.), *The Amsterdam School, Dutch Expressionist Architecture, 1915-1930*, New York and Cambridge, Mass., 1983.
Wollin, Nils G., *Modern Swedish Decorative Art*, London, 1931.

OTHER PLACES

James, Cary, *Frank Lloyd Wright's Imperial Hotel*, New York, 1968.

Tokyo Metropolitan Teien Art Museum, *The Building and Its History*, Tokyo, 1987.

ART DECO REVIVAL

Anagyros, Sophie, *Intérieurs: Le Mobilier Français 1980 . . .*, Paris, 1983.

Capella, Juli and Larres, Quim, *Designed by Architects in the 1980s*, London, 1988.

Horn, Richard, *Memphis Objects, Furniture & Patterns*, New York, 1988.
Hulanicki, Barbara, *From A to Biba*, London, 1983.

Radice, Barbara, *Memphis*, New York, 1984.
Rousseau, François Olivier, *Andrée Putman*, London, 1990.

Wheeler, Karen Vogel; Arnell, Peter and Bickford, Ted (eds.), *Michael Graves: Buildings and Projects 1966-1981*, New York, 1983.

PERIODICALS AND JOURNALS

In the 1910s, 1920s and 1930s a weath of journals – monthly, annual, short-lived and long-established – published photographs, articles and reviews relating to Art Deco objects and interiors, either commentaries on salons and exhibitions, or visits to actual apartments or houses. The following lists include a selection of international publications from the Art Deco period, some of which are still published, as well as modern magazines which often feature articles on Art Deco design and interiors.

FRANCE
L'Amour de l'Art
Architecture
L'Architecture Vivant
L'Art d'Aujourd'hui
L'Art Décoratif
Art et Décoration
Art et Industrie
Art-Goût-Beauté
L'Art Vivant
Les Arts de la Maison
Cahiers d'Art
La Demeure Française
L'Esprit Nouveau
Feuillets d'Art
L'Illustration
Mobilier et Décoration d'Intérieur
La Renaissance de l'Art Français

GERMANY
Dekorative Kunst
Deutsche Kunst und Dekoration
Die Kunst
Kunst und Handwerk
Zeitschrift für Innen-Dekoration

GREAT BRITAIN
The Architectural Review
Country Life
Decoration
Harper's Bazaar
House and Garden
Our Homes and Gardens
The Studio
The Studio Year Book of Decorative Art
Vogue

UNITED STATES
American Magazine of Art
The Architectural Record
Creative Art
Design
Good Furniture Magazine
Good Furniture and Decoration
Harper's Bazaar
Home and Field
House and Garden
Interiors
Vogue

BELGIUM
L'Art Moderne

ITALY
Domus

THE NETHERLANDS
De Stijl
Wendingen

AUSTRALIA
The Home

POST-1940 AND/OR EXISTENT PUBLICATIONS
The Antique Collector
Architectural Digest
Art & Antiques
Connaissance des Arts
The Connoisseur (now *Connoisseur*)
L'Estampille
Jardin des Arts
The Antiques Magazine
L'Oeil
Réalités
The World of Interiors

INDEX

INDEX

INDEX